TO: Norman + Lou...

Then [barcode] ...

for me [D1193248]

you most

Love you,

Fran

Frances S. Peterson

Isaiah 26:3

The Eagle and the Egret

The Eagle and the Egret

By Frances L. Peterson

Four Seasons Publishers
Titusville, FL

The Eagle and the Egret

For information contact Four Seasons Publishers
P.O.Box 51, Titusville, FL 32781

④

PRINTING HISTORY
First Printing 2006

ISBN 1-932497-05-6

PRINTED IN THE UNITED STATES OF AMERICA
1 2 3 4 5 6 7 8 9 10

Foreword

We knew Fran and her first husband, Kedar Bryan, for several years before he died in 1974. Their story is told in Fran's second book, *A Tale of Two Bamboos*. They lived all over the Far East during their thirty-two-year marriage and had one extraordinary adventure after another.

At The Church of the Saviour, we saw her go from deep sorrow in her shattering loss of Kedar to acceptance, and in the end, finding that life is good as it is given. She found a home, family, and renewal in this community of faith.

In God's perfect time she met and married Pete, Col. C. R. Peterson, USAF. Their move to Florida didn't separate their hearts from us, and within two years they volunteered to serve with COSIGN (Church of the Saviour International Good Neighbors), a relief effort for the refugees streaming over the border into Thailand from Laos, Cambodia, and Vietnam.

That was just the beginning of their service wherever called, spending their time and treasure as God gave them strength. One opportunity followed another for twenty-five happy years. They hold that the secret mission of older adults is to leave a legacy of redemptive power to incorporate our values for future generations.

If any of us "of a certain age" might be inclined to become just another retiree on the golf course, be forewarned. *The Eagle and the Egret* is the true story of two newlywed seniors called beyond their comfort zone into God's next adventure. Reading it will challenge the idea that God might not be finished with *any* of us yet.

Mary Campbell Cosby
Co-founder
Church of the Saviour
Washington D.C

The Eagle and the Egret

is dedicated to

Pete

my

beloved.

The Eagle and the Egret

Introduction

Fran

Hi, welcome to my world!

I'm a "mish-kid," born and raised in North Korea. My parents, Henry and Ruth Lampe, were Presbyterian missionaries in Korea before the country was divided. Our home was in Syenchun, fifty miles south of the Yalu River.

There were eight of us little Lampes, four boys and four girls. Our parents did their math well. I was number six, and the third daughter, thus my first book, *Journal of the Third Daughter, Growing up in Korea.* Mother home-schooled us with the Calvert System; then one by one as we reached the sixth grade we went off to Pyeng Yang Foreign School in Pyeng Yang, now the North Korean capital. It was a mission-run boarding school for children of foreigners from all over the Far

East, providing a first class education in preparation for colleges and universities in the States.

I met Kedar Bryan from Shanghai aboard the *Heian Maru* as we pulled out of Yokohama harbor, on the way to college. We were going to different schools, so although the attraction was strong we parted as good friends, nothing more.

We kept in touch, and after WW II started we talked seriously about getting married and did so on October 31, 1942.

Kedar went into the Marine Corps and was sent to the South Pacific, and I moved to St. Louis to be with my parents and bore his son, Edwin Kedar Bryan. The story of our life during and after the war then all over the Far East is told in my second book, *A Tale of Two Bamboos*. In Shanghai we had two more children, moved forty-two times, three of which were evacuations. We lived in China, Korea, Japan (briefly), the States, India, Hong Kong, Singapore, Thailand, and Vietnam.

Kedar's lung cancer was discovered when we were in Saigon. He died eighteen months later, and I was a widow for four years before I married Pete, and we moved to Florida to begin our new life together.

Conrad R. Peterson
Pete

Pete first opened his big blue eyes on November 1, 1916, in an apartment above a bank on Main Street in Coleraine, Minnesota. Had he been born a few minutes earlier, on October 31, he'd have been a goblin, but by holding off he arrived on All Saints' Day.

The attending physician was in a hurry and failed to ask what his name would be. For some reason he wrote Cecil Eugene Peterson. Nobody liked it, and his parents decided to change it to Conrad Reginald Peterson, Connie for short. While in the service he was known as "Pete," but it wasn't until after he'd retired that he took school records to the courthouse and had the change made official.

His childhood was typical—happy and full of challenges. His older sister, Carol, left home for nurses' training before he was in his teens, and Denton, several years younger, was sickly. He spent a year in bed with osteomyelitis. Pete was of average height but took on all comers who gave his younger brother any grief.

He loved all kinds of sports. He was in great demand in church choirs and school musicals as his bass voice developed.

Early in 1941 he and his sweetheart, Babe (Gloria Wood) eloped and kept it secret for several months.

Their daughter, Bonnie, was born on December 17th in St. Luke's Hospital in St. Louis.

That same year Pete and several of his friends with high draft numbers decided to enlist, choosing the Army Air Corps. The evening they arrived at Jefferson Barracks, Missouri, with a lot of other recruits, they were lined up on the railroad station platform and given the usual greeting from the top sergeant, who let them know in no uncertain terms that they were the sorriest looking bunch of humanity he'd ever seen.

"Does anybody here know how to pound a typewriter?" he bellowed. Pete raised his hand. "Report to my office first thing in the morning," he commanded. For the six weeks of basic training when the rest of the grunts were marching, drilling, sweating, and aching in every muscle and joint, he sat in a comfortable office typing up rosters of those going to schools all over the country. When he found that the last of his friends was to attend radio school and didn't want to be left behind, he typed his name at the bottom of the list and was gone. He's always wondered what the sergeant thought when he didn't show up for work.

One assignment followed another punctuated by schools and training sessions that advanced him steadily from buck private to captain by the end of the war.

"I never had an assignment I didn't like," Pete said, "though some were better than others." The closest he came to combat was on submarine patrol duty off the coast of California.

"One night at the end of our patrol," he recalled, "the cloud cover was very heavy all the way to the ground. We couldn't fly under it to get back to San Diego. Everything was pitch black, and we couldn't locate a landing field because the West Coast was on total blackout. Fuel was running low. I radioed that we were in trouble and without a fix would have to ditch in the ocean. Just as we began that final run a searchlight went up, piercing a break in the clouds. The pilot rolled over on his left wing and followed the shaft of light to a safe landing at the air base. As we taxied up to the hangar, the engines of our B-24 coughed and died. They were bone-dry."

Later in Barksdale, Loisiana, he was a member of a B-26 instructor crew. Every fourth to sixth Sunday morning they flew a mission to improve their skills. On one such day when he reported to the field, some enlisted pilots were there for a test flight.

"Pete, are you willing to give up your place for these fellows and take the day off?" the instructor asked.

"Gladly!" he answered, picked up his family, and went to church. The plane was no more than airborne when it lost power and crashed, killing all aboard!

Whenever Pete was in one place long enough, Babe and Bonnie joined him, and back they'd go to

Virginia, Minnesota, when he was off on another assignment. On very short stints Babe left Bonnie with her grandparents and went alone to be with Pete.

He was assigned to Alaska twice, once during the war and the second time just after it ended. He was in charge of navigational aids, radio range, and air traffic control.

Pete spent eight years in nuclear testing on Johnston Island; Eniwoetok; Bikini; Washington, D.C.; and Sandia Base; New Mexico; three years in Germany as assistant director of plans; two years in French Morocco at Sidi Slimane as squadron director of operations for AACS (Airways and Air Communications Service); three years in Turkey with NATO as director of plans and programs; and finally arrived at Hanscom Field, Massachusetts, where he directed the establishment of AUTOVON, a worldwide communications system for the U.S. government and military.

From time to time Pete told me about some of the funny and strange things he encountered. While in Germany his unit was establishing north-south path propagation for world communications. He was negotiating with the British for a southern terminal in the Aden Protectorate. In time he went to have a look at the receiver site and found that at high tide it was under water! The corresponding transmitter site was in

Yemen's territory, and when the tribal chief wouldn't let him in to have a look, the whole deal was canceled. Instead, they were able to colocate with the U.S. Army Signal Corps in Eritrea, Ethiopia.

During the time Pete was stationed at Johnston Island, he went to Hawaii for R&R. Once he and four or five others booked the penthouse suite at the Waikiki Beach Hotel for the weekend.

Lo and behold, a huge bridge tournament was on with generous prizes for the winners. Those fellows played bridge every night and believed they were expert enough to take on anyone and win.

Pete and his friend, John, signed up and were put at a table with two white-haired ladies. Delighted, they just knew they'd be able to take them to the cleaners. How wrong they were! Looking sweet and innocent, they took Pete and John to the woodshed, and they were glad to leave the tournament with shirts on and dignity intact.

When atmospheric nuclear tests were being concluded on Johnston Island in 1962, a near disaster took place that changed Pete's life forever. All the top brass were there to observe the shot. It was a really big deal. A short time after takeoff at 2:00 a.m. the range safety officer shouted, "Destroy! Destroy!" The missile had gone erratic. It was directly overhead, and they faced the very real possibility that everything on the island would be blown up as debris rained down on them. Twelve fully loaded twin engine planes were on the taxi strip ready to take off to gather radiation samples after the detonation; twenty rocket launchers on the southwest shore stood fueled and ready to fire. Nearby were liquid oxygen tanks and structures housing the whole operation.

Pete left the command post and went to his office, put his head down on his desk, and prayed. A very clear message came to him from the Lord.

"Pete, I'm in charge here. Do not be afraid. It will be all right." He went back to join the others and said he was confident it would be okay. Naturally they thought he was out of his mind, but they waited.

They were underground and could hear nothing, but on the closed-circuit TV they saw debris falling on the lighted areas of the island. When they were sure it was clear, Pete sent the rad-safe team out to see what had happened. They were astonished to see that *nothing* had been hit. It all fell between buildings and on the runway or beside the planes and rolled under them. There was no detectable radiation. Later it was discovered that all of it had fallen in the lagoon! Pete was never the same after that.

He retired in 1970. He and Babe moved to Albuquerque, New Mexico, where they built the house of their dreams up in the heights, overlooking the city.

He took several jobs but ended up with GTE Lenkert and stayed for several years. Finally he'd had enough; they sold the house, bought an Air Stream trailer and a Chrysler wagon to pull it, and set off to see the U.S. of A. With their wanderlust satiated, they returned to Albuquerque to settle down. Bonnie was happily married and had two little ones. Life was good.

They put money down on a townhouse, ordered kitchen and laundry equipment delivered from Sears, and retrieved their household goods from storage. They were moving the kitchen things from the trailer into the condo when Babe complained of a terrible headache. An hour and a half later she died of what was believed to be a cerebral hemorrhage. What a shock! He had no interest in staying there without her. Everything went back into storage. He sold the trailer and drove to Augusta, Georgia, to be with Bonnie, Luke, and the children. That's where he was two years later when our friends Peggy Jones and Milley Grimm invited him to come to Peggy's wedding. She was marrying my brother Jim. The man for Fran!

From Meeting to Marriage

Meeting Pete for the first time was nice. Both Milley and Peggy had known him and his wife, Babe, for years and thought he was a good person for me to know. A year and a half after his wife's death, he was off in Mississippi playing golf with friends when he got a call from Peggy urging him to come to her wedding and meet her new sister-in-law. Being a trusting soul, he headed north for the big day.

I liked Pete right away, but it was by no means love at first sight. He smoked, and when I saw him for the first time he was exhaling a long drag. The thought that popped in my mind was, Oh no! I'm not going there again. Kedar's smoking ended his life.

Pete was there to meet me, so we spent as much time together as we could in the middle of a festive, joyful occasion with lots of friends and food. After three days and many hours later, we parted, anticipating future times together.

Letters and phone calls followed, but the possibility of a serious romance wasn't a reality for some time. I was working hard on a couple of courses in George Mason University's night school, and there was a constant worry over my son Edwin's drinking problem. Oh how I longed for Kedar's good common sense to help me. He could always see things with a clearer head than I, and I missed him.

I regularly attended open AA meetings and heard recovering alcoholics tell of the depths to which they had fallen before they got help and rebuilt their lives. I hung on every word, every hope, and prayed that it would happen for Edwin too. Time and again I paid for his admission to a twenty-eight-day treatment facility only to have him head for the nearest ABC store fifteen minutes after his release, but I couldn't help aiding him any way I could. I was as sick as he was.

After one particularly bad time, I was able to get him admitted to Safety Harbor in Greensboro, North Carolina. There was a combination work and treatment program which seemed to be effective. He was pleased with the job he secured in a counseling program. With his degree in psychology, it was a good fit.

When Edwin came to McLean for Peggy and Jim's wedding he looked wonderful. Nobody could be more delightful than he when he was sober. He told me he'd met Linda Reavis and wanted to marry her. She was teaching school, and they met when she interviewed him for a paper she was writing about rehabilitation. I wasn't sure he was ready to make any serious commitment, but then he wasn't asking for my advice. All I could do was pray, and I did—a lot.

Two months later, on June 14, Edwin and Linda were married by my brother, Willard Lampe, in the Presbyterian Church in Edenton, North Carolina. My son Jim and his wife, Donna, came down from New Hampshire, and we drove on together. We got there before the bridal couple and her family and friends, and when they arrived I could see right away that things were not going well. Edwin was three sheets to the wind, but we had a couple of hours to get him sobered up enough to get through the day. The whole thing made me heartsick for both of them. What should have been a glorious celebration was a disaster waiting to happen.

Edwin was accepted in the nurses' training school in Greensboro, which pleased both of us. He always had a servant's heart, and what better way to exercise his gifts than in nursing. When I asked him what he'd like to have for a birthday present, he chose a subscription to a nursing magazine. I gave a sigh of relief. Things were looking up.

In the meantime, Pete and I were feeling the need to be together to sort things out if we were to go forward with our relationship, so I took a week off from work and flew down to South Carolina, where he met me; and we drove to Hilton Head.

When it's your "second time around" you know a little better which questions to ask. While we walked the beach one morning talking about finances, I said, "I've always believed in tithing my income. How about you?"

"Oh sure," he answered, "and I'm one of the big spenders when it comes to the church. Last year I gave a total of $350."

"Well, that's not exactly what I'm talking about," I said. "A tithe, as I understand it, is 10 percent of your gross income. For as long as I can remember, Mother and Daddy were very careful to tithe their missionary salary, and believe me it wasn't large. But they always had more than enough. Tithing is also practiced in the Church of the Saviour where I belong, and I really do believe in it. In Malachi 3:10 it says, 'Bring all the tithes into the storehouse so that there will be food enough in my Temple; if you do, I will open up the windows of heaven for you and pour out a blessing so great you won't have room enough to take it in!' It's the only place in the Bible where we are asked to put God to the test."

"I'll give it some serious thought," he said after making a few quick calculations.

"Look, honey, it's your money, and you do what you think is best. All I'm saying is that any income I have, I'll tithe. Is that okay with you?"

"Well of course," he agreed. "We'll work it out. Don't worry." And I didn't.

As we talked about the things that mattered to us, our likes and dislikes, hopes and visions for the future, everything seemed to mesh seamlessly. On top of that, Pete was such an easy person to be with. Always a gentleman, never cursing or using course language. It was a pleasure to be in his company. I could find no fault except maybe the smoking, but I hoped that in time he'd give it up.

Before heading back north we sat down to talk about the big question, and the answer was, yes indeed, let's get married! And so it was on March 22, 1978, we pledged each to the other our love and commitment from that day forward.

We drove to the nearest airport so I could fly home, but I might have done just as well without a plane and floated back. We set no wedding date, but that would be done soon.

April 12, I remembered as I awakened that it was my daughter-in-law Donna's birthday. I'd call her in the evening. A full day at the office was followed with a trip into the District to meet my mission group and serve in the Potter's House coffee house for three hours. Just as I was getting into bed the phone rang; it was Edwin's wife, Linda.

"Are you sitting down?" she asked. (I didn't like the sound of that. It meant bad news.)

"Yes, I am," I answered, "What can I do for you?"

"Edwin is dead."

"How did it happen?"

"He shot himself last night." For a moment I couldn't speak, shocked as I was by the emotion that swept over me—praise God it's over; the agony is over! He suffered so much in his battle with depression and alcohol. He seemed to have no hope that things would ever get any better. At last he was at peace, but at what cost!

I talked briefly with her and said I'd be down the next day. The gears shifted, and I went on automatic pilot as I made calls to my officemate to tell her I'd not be in the next day. I called my brother Jim, who also lived in McLean, and he came right away. He put through a call to my daughter, Anne, who lived in Montana, and gave her the news. I called my son Jim and Donna and Mother Bryan. The others could be told later.

As the numbness gave way to reality, the enormity of our loss became real. Sobs racked me as the tears flowed. Was there no end to the pain? My precious son, my firstborn, handsome, bright, with every possibility there for the taking! What went wrong? What did I do to hurt him? Oh, my wonderful son, why? Where did I fail you? The questions went on and on, but there were no answers, just death. There was a ten-pound, hard, aching knot in my chest that I rubbed, but it didn't go away. It just sat there making my hands and feet feel heavy, too.

When I called Pete in the morning he said he'd drive to Greensboro and meet me there. Jim came over, and we made the trip together. Bless his heart, Jim, the kid who tormented the socks off of me when we were children, turned out to be a tower of strength every time my life hit a snag.

He was director of personnel at the Eastern Division of the American Red Cross. When things had to be done, he knew what questions to ask and how to cut through red tape. He followed up with the mortuary, the things Linda wanted, found out where Edwin's car was and was able to claim it, and tended to other nuts-and-bolts matters.

Pete found us, and it was such a relief to have both him and Jim there. Pete had already checked into a motel, but at about 10:00 when Jim and I needed rooms, it took us over an hour of calling to find just one. Because the Furniture Mart was on that weekend, everything was taken, but we finally located one that had two beds, they said, but no towels, so Linda gave us some. The key was at the desk. They gave it to us after we paid, and what a room! There was one very small double bed with sheets and pillows. The bathroom ceiling was host to generous amounts of black mold clinging to its broken tiles. Get the picture? But there was nothing else, and we were so tired we didn't care.

Brother Willard and his wife, Charlotte, drove over from Edenton to conduct the funeral service. Students and staff came in uniform from the nursing school as well as the director of Safety Harbor. They all liked and appreciated Edwin so much and were devastated and saddened at the tragic loss. It was good to meet the people about whom he'd spoken so enthusiastically.

That was a period when something big happened every month.

On May 18 Jimmy's wife, Donna, had open-heart surgery. Born with a congenital heart problem, it was her fourth operation to close a hole that leaked good blood with every beat. Since she and Jim were married, she'd suffered several miscarriages, and in trying to find the reason, tests revealed the corrective patch on her heart had broken away, so the baby wasn't getting properly oxygenated blood and couldn't survive.

Donna was not at all sure anybody could live through four such procedures, but her doctor (who'd worked with Dr. Christian Bernard of South Africa) assured her it was no problem. She'd feel like whipping her weight in wildcats in six weeks. Everything went just as the doctor said, but instead of tangling with wildcats, she was out water skiing. We were all thanking God for answered prayers.

In June we went to Florida to find a place to call home. At first Pete asked where I'd like to live, and immediately I suggested the Washington, D.C., area. I loved my little nest on the tenth floor of McLean House— too small for two but we could probably swap it for a larger one. His answer was a firm "no way." He'd spent enough time in the Pentagon to know he never wanted to live anywhere near it again, so I asked what his choice would be. Just as quickly he suggested central Florida. I had never been there. He had lots of friends in that area, so we went to the Farrells' in Cocoa Beach and spent a week looking. We didn't want a house. We wanted to be free to come and go without the responsibility of yard work.

"It's not my bag," Pete said, nor was it mine. With my "purple thumb" I kill everything but philodendron. We also decided on no dogs, cats, birds, or fish— anything that would miss us if we went away for any length of time. Soon we narrowed it down to three condos, and finally chose 443 Dove Lane in Satellite Beach. It was an 1800-square-foot, two-story condo on a canal with a boat dock. We put down a deposit, ordered an upgrade on the carpet, and went back home feeling very proud of ourselves—and we set our wedding date for September 16, 1978.

For several months I had a feeling of fullness in my lower throat. It started out as a mild infection that was quickly cleared up with medication, but the pressure continued. One doctor said it was probably stress as my life had been anything but tranquil. He suggested that at work, when I had a few free moments, I should lower my head between my knees and relax. I tried it, but it didn't help.

About that time I saw a "60 Minutes" program about research showing that people who'd received X-ray in the head/neck area in the 1940s should be examined to see if their thyroid was free of problems. Right away I thought of my son Jim, who'd received X-ray therapy for his enlarged thymus when he was a baby. Perhaps he should get it checked out.

"Mom," he said, "that program was on months ago. You saw the rerun, and yes, I did get it checked. I'm fine. Don't worry."

All of this made me remember that during that same time I'd received X-ray therapy for a very irritating rash on the back of my head. I took a couple of hours of leave and went across the river to the George Washington Hospital to sign myself in at the radiology department for a thyroid examination. The nurse never questioned a thing, and it wasn't until she'd given me an intravenous injection of radioactive isotopes that she asked which doctor had sent me.

"I came on my own," I told her. "No doctor sent me, but I'm here because I want to know if this fullness I feel at the bottom of my throat has anything to do with my thyroid." As she sputtered in protest, I told her about the research by Dr. Concanin in Allegheny General Hospital in Pittsburgh concerning thyroid problems. I fit the profile.

Since I had already been injected there was nothing to do but go ahead with the examination, and sure enough, two tumors showed up!

On July 19 Pete was there to hold my hand as they wheeled me into surgery and by my side afterwards to tell me everything was fine. The tumors were out and there was no cancer. Home free! Wow, it was getting awfully close to our wedding date, and there was still a lot to do!

All my brothers and sisters came for the big day except for Heydon, the oldest of the eight siblings and his wife, Mary, who were on a tour in Europe. My Anne and Jim took part in the ceremony as did Pete's daughter, Bonnie, and her husband, Luke.

For me, the sanctuary of the Church of the Saviour is a sacred place. There I knelt and spoke my vows for membership in that community of believers as all in the congregation laid hands on me by proxy. It was there that four years and eight days earlier we celebrated Kedar's home-going, and now in that same place before the rough-hewn cross, I was exchanging wedding vows with Pete. My heart was full to overflowing, remembering and letting go of the past and placing my hand in Pete's big one, trusting God for every good thing in our future.

Col. & Mrs. C.R. Peterson

At Home in Florida

Everything was new. It had that special look, smell, and feel. Pete put up shelves in the closet; I lined the cupboards with paper, and one by one we unpacked the boxes and put away things or laid them to rest in the "what-shall-we-do-with-this?" pile.

After about two weeks Pete had had enough and went out to golf with his friends. Wonderful! There's nothing nicer than a guy who's spent some time with his friends, vented his frustrations on that little white ball, and gotten in a few of those really sweet shots that feel just right when the balls go where you aim them. Ah, life was good.

I shall forever be thankful to the U.S. Air Force. By the time I got Pete he was well trained—no clothes on the floor, the toothpaste cap always in place. When I went down to fix breakfast, he made the bed, and he knew enough to stay out of the kitchen when I was cooking. As Peggy used to say, "It's a one-butt kitchen."

He'd set the table when we were having a party and didn't dust but pushed the vacuum cleaner around. I tell you what—we were a team.

We had our disagreements, but they were unimportant, and we mostly laughed them away. There was always laughter, and that keeps you healthy, I'm told.

Pete took care of accounts, and I was happy to give up that chore. Doing them was my hardest adjustment to widowhood, and I was pleased that he liked the job. Our desks were side by side in the den, and one day when he was paying bills, I saw a check he'd written for the interest on a credit card.

"You have credit-card debt?" I asked in disbelief.

"Sure, no problem," he answered, "I write off the interest when I pay my taxes."

"I can't believe it," I shot back. "That's pennies on the dollar. Pete, how big is the debt?" When he told me I just about died. That was one time we didn't laugh away our difference. My mish-kid upbringing kicked in, and we had it out. He always had a good check coming in and didn't worry about debt. He paid off the interest, and when he wanted something, he just got it and worried about it later. The "easy come, easy go" probably started after he lost Babe, but I wasn't happy about it.

Bless his heart, he was shocked that I took such a strong stand against carrying debt and in six months had it all paid off. I was very relieved.

"How about giving 5 percent to the church to see how it goes?" he said at about the same time.

"That's fine, honey. Do what seems good to you."

A couple of months later he brought up the subject again.

"I never missed the 5 percent, so I'm going for 10." He also delighted in raising our contribution every time he got an increase.

A few years later when interest rates were tumbling, we looked into refinancing our 9.75-percent mortgage, but by then we had enough to pay it off. That felt really good, and we celebrated.

It's said that when you move to Florida, your friends and family do not forsake you. True. In short order all of them came to check us out. We in turn put hundreds of miles on our car visiting them.

We enjoyed a great sense of freedom. We gave keys to neighbors to check on our condo to make sure all was okay, particularly after a hurricane. We loaded up Pete's big Chrysler with golf clubs and clothes, and off we went. He drove and I read aloud. We devoured such books as Colleen McColloogh's *TheThorn Birds, Taipan,* and everything else written by James Clavel. Malcom Smith's series on Africa was wonderful.

One night we stopped at Cordele, Georgia, and asked the clerk at the motel desk about a place to eat.

"Oh," she said, "We got a good one. Turn right outa here, go one block, then hang a left. Go two blocks to the Cracker Barrel. They'll feed you up good." We laughed all the way there. We were hooked, and whenever we were on the road and there was a Cracker Barrel within shout'n distance near mealtime, we stopped there.

There was great comfort in being married to Pete. In my first marriage I was a very dependent wife, modeled for me by my mother. She was the undisputed boss in the home, but Daddy was the strong one whose word was the final. They never seemed to argue about anything. I found the answer later when I asked her how they managed strong disagreements, which surely they must have had. "We worked them out in private, and your dad didn't always have his way," she assured me.

Kedar took care of the finances and invested wisely, but I hadn't a clue what we had or where it was until just before he died. Reality set in. I did a good job but never enjoyed it. It was a heavy weight that had to be borne.

That was one of the best parts of being married to Pete. He had a good head for numbers, and I happily handed everything over to him. It was a huge relief to let it all go, even though I'd done well.

It was wonderful to be loved and needed. The comfort of belonging took away the pain of separation for those four years when my life felt unfocused and incomplete.

I liked my job and was on a track for moving out of the secretarial pool into management. My social life was active, and the Church of the Saviour challenged me at every turn to grow in fellowship within my mission group and in prayer and meditation for closer walk with our Lord.

In some ways as a widow I had a wonderful sense of freedom. Old routines didn't bind me. In my leisure I could do just as I pleased. Didn't want to cook dinner? I didn't. The day's fine? Forget the dusting, cleaning, and laundry and just take off for a drive or a walk through the mall. All that other stuff could wait for another time. But I'd give everything up for Pete. What a nice guy, a gentleman in every sense of the word. He loved me but didn't smother me. He wanted me to be near but did not pester with small talk. He was thoughtful and kind and had only good things to say about others. Was he perfect? Well, almost, but perfect for me.

The empty nest has its merits. Privacy and uninterrupted sleep times are good. Our sex lives when we were young were more energetic than in later years, but being in our seventies and eighties was surprising.

An early morning half-awake snuggle could turn into sweet, gentle lovemaking. After a morning of golf, a light lunch, a shower and cat-nap, the stage was set for a rollicking romp in the hay, and at the end of a romantic evening together, pure joy with each other was a special gift. Ah, yes!

At home in Satellite Beach

Thailand 1980

One evening at a Christian Businessmen's meeting, Pete and I both felt the need to request a prayer for guidance. We'd been married for a year and a half, were enjoying the good life of golf, bridge, cruises, and visits with friends and family. We sang in our church choir and delivered for Meals on Wheels, but we missed the challenge of doing something beyond our comfort zone.

The speaker laid his hands on us, and in effect scolded us for not using our gifts in a larger way. That was a surprise, but it also answered a nagging question—is there something more we should be doing? That night we began praying that if this was God's idea, to please let us know, and we'd be obedient. Now that's taking a big risk if you really mean it.

Within the week we received a call from the Church of the Saviour in Washington, D.C., where I was a member before marrying Pete. Their calling is to minister to the poor of the city. When they learned of the crisis in Thailand, where people were pouring over the borders from Laos and Cambodia in the north and arriving by sea from Vietnam on the southern coast near the border with Malaysia, COSIGN (Church of the Saviour International Good Neighbors) was born. The world was shocked, horrified by the tales of brutality and genocide coming from countries overrun by the Communists.

Directed by Helen Carry and Elizabeth O'Conor, COSIGN decided to lend its weight to the massive assistance by sponsoring volunteers to work with refugees. Headquarters were in Bangkok under the leadership of Jerry Aitken, a Seventh Day Adventist missionary. He was able to provide housing and a place to get started in whatever camps were assigned by the United Nations High Commission for Refugees (UNHCR).

In Ubon in the northeast they were to teach English to Lao refugees who'd be going to the U.S. or any other English-speaking country. At Songkhla in the south where the Vietnamese arrived in their small canal boats, COSIGN volunteers were assigned construction work, digging wells, and teaching English.

Money to support the effort was sent to whoever was at the headquarters management in Bangkok. The turnover of volunteers was heavy because everybody wanted to be in one of the camps where the action was.

Pete and I let it be known that we were available to go with the understanding that we'd stay in Bangkok. Pete's job would be to put the books in order, and I'd be responsible for hospitality as volunteers came and went. Usually they stayed anywhere from six weeks to six months. Young adults gave a summer vacation, a semester from college, or time before going to work after college. Retirees like ourselves went too—folks of every type and description who wanted to do something for those desperately needy people. Our departure date was September 1, 1980.

We had no idea how long we'd be gone, so we invited Mary and Art Baird, friends from Ohio, to use our place in Florida, where they could keep their boat in the canal right behind our condo. They were more than delighted to take us up on the offer, and we were just as pleased to have our residence occupied by good friends.

As plans developed we shared our hopes and aspirations with friends at Trinity Presbyterian Church. Dennis Bennett, our pastor, encouraged us to go to represent them, promising support as needed, and covering in prayer.

On July 7 we started out in our VW camper on a two-month trip up the East Coast to Maine, across Canada, and down the West Coast to Los Angeles, visiting friends and family along the way. There were several events that I will forever connect with that trip. While in Quebec having lunch in a revolving restaurant atop a hotel, we witnessed a thunder storm from above! It was a bright, sunny day with occasional clouds passing below us. Sidewalk restaurants were doing a brisk business when a rain cloud moved in, letting loose a heavy shower, and lightning forked to the ground. Umbrellas blew every which way, and patrons ran for cover.

We camped near Banff with Anne, Gery, and their children, Lisa and David. In a day or two we needed food and found a big Safeway in town. I was surprised at what we discovered on every aisle. Tucked away on the shelves were opened and partly eaten foods of every sort: Twinkies, cookies, candy bars, lunch meats, celery sticks, cheeses, ice cream bar wrappers, soda pop and milk! Summer vacations draw hikers and bikers north, and it would seem that some got their food where they could without having to pay for it. I never saw anything like it before or since. The store must have lost a ton of money.

While we were camping I asked Pete to open a bottle that I couldn't manage, and in doing so he clenched his teeth. The tooth that got a lot of pressure was the one in the front on a bridge that had a porcelain facing—and out it popped! Oh my. I got out some Super Glue that worked initially but not for long. Fortunately vanity was not one of his traits.

Two days before departure for Thailand, we stopped in at McCord Air Base to do some last-minute shopping and get our required gamma globulin shots. I noticed a dental clinic and suggested we try it for Pete's tooth job.

"No," he insisted. "They're always booked up weeks ahead, and there's no way they can fix it anyway." I didn't think there was any harm in asking, so while he waited in the car I took our ID cards and asked for emergency help. What do you know! There had just been a cancellation, and a man who could do the job was free. In an hour the old boy had a tooth that was as good as new. "See what can happen when you ask?" I teased.

Several times on the trip the camper lost power on the hills, but no garage could locate the problem, so we kept going. Most of the time it was fine. Phil and Marjorie Dunham, longtime friends of Pete's who lived in Los Angeles, agreed to keep the car while we were gone, and Phil said he'd get the problem fixed. Thank the Lord.

On September 1 we were off on our big adventure. Going with the sun made for a very long day. We arrived in Bangkok at 2:00 a.m. but nobody was there to meet us. That was okay; I knew the general area where the compound was located. We got a taxi and went into town. The driver didn't have a clue (many Bangkok taxi drivers are farmers who need extra money), and after driving around for a half hour, I told him to go to the Rex Hotel, where we spent the rest of the night. The next day we called the Aitkens to let them know we'd arrived and where we were. They were full of apologies when they checked the cablegram and realized they had misread it and expected us the next day.

Bangkok wasn't new for me as Kedar and I'd lived there for three years in the 1960s, but Pete wasn't quite so ready for some of the challenges. After taking over the bookkeeping, he decided to open an account in a neighborhood Thai bank. They were very happy to take COSIGN's money, but there was no way to write checks. You want money, you go to the bank and draw it out. He wasn't happy with the arrangement, but what to do? When in Rome.

COSIGN records didn't exist. Pete was shown a large drawer full of receipts, mostly in Thai, and that was it! He found somebody to translate and got them all in order. From what he could gather, the money was well spent, but there were several generous donors who needed to know that when filing their tax returns. He set up an accounting system, figured what money needed to go where, and was the one who dispensed it. One morning after a particularly frustrating encounter at the bank, Pete stormed into our room.

"All I need is a tee time at Patrick golf course tomorrow morning at eight o'clock. I've had it with these people," he announced.

The proximity of the bank wasn't really all that important, but communication was. I suggested we talk to the people at the Bank of America, located on the other side of the city on the ground floor of the building where I worked with Utah-Martin-Day during the Vietnam War. It meant a long bus ride, but it was the best thing we ever did. There were American managers and staff, and being understood was just what Pete needed. After the transfer, he had a checkbook, and life was sweet and reasonable again!

COSIGN was given an apartment in a duplex. We had three bedrooms and a full bath upstairs and a living room, dining room, bath, and kitchen downstairs. Pete and I had one bedroom, and the other two were for single women or couples. Downstairs were accommodations for men. There were four beds, but if more were needed, there was a big stack of futons in one corner and bedding in a closet. Some nights we took care of eighteen. All those coming and going were with us for just a few days, so it worked well.

The Aitken family—Jerry, Judy, Jay, Jolene, and Julie—lived in the other side, and we had all our meals with them. What a blessing that was for me—no grocery shopping and cooking in hot, steamy Bangkok.

Contract flights for the refugees came out of Los Angeles empty, so COSIGN arranged for our volunteers to travel on them for fifty dollars apiece. Nice. They always arrived at 2:00 a.m. We picked them up, showed them the bathroom and where they were to sleep and told them we'd see them at breakfast next door. Most of them had gone through twelve time zones and were bright-eyed and raring to go at eight o'clock.

Frequently there were volunteers for other agencies that were not met (we knew the feeling); we took them home with us and gave them a place to sleep and breakfast before calling their sponsors. Most had never been overseas and were touchingly thankful.

Our volunteers were eager to do and see everything, so off we went by bus to take care of their needs. Money had to be exchanged, and if it was too much for Pete's stash we went to the bank. Likewise, one of the first orders of business was to get them registered at the U.S. embassy. Because it usually took until noon we went to a nice cool, clean, air-conditioned hotel coffee shop for lunch and then back to the house. Without fail they wanted to go sight-seeing, but I knew better. By the time we reached our compound they were ready to crash and sleep the clock around. I loved these kids. They were so predictable.

Ubon in the north was an overnight train trip, and to Songkhla in the south, it took eighteen hours. They had bench seats that were made up into sleepers at night—complete with sheets, blankets, and pillows. After a few days of adjusting and seeing Bangkok, we loaded up the volunteers with food for the trip and some extras for the folks already at the camps. They always pleaded for more peanut butter and jam, and we sent it to them by the bucketful. Guess what they were raised on!

Just before the train pulled out I took the women to check out the bathroom arrangements. There was no toilet, only a "squatty-potty." There are two foot prints on a floor-level porcelain structure with a hole between. It flushed and was clean, so what more could you want? You provided your own toilet tissue.

"What's that?" they asked, pointing.

"That's the john" I explained. "You put your feet on the two prints, drop your drawers, hunker down and take care of business. Here's a roll of paper. It's really a good arrangement, and you'll get used to it, honestly."

"You didn't tell us about such a thing," they protested. I hurried off the train as it began to move, glad they didn't have time to get off too! Pete never failed to get a kick out of their reaction, and we laughed all the way home. Poor kids, but they learned quickly.

One day we had word from our Ubon people that they needed several kinds of books for the English language program and better cooking arrangements. On one charcoal stove the cook was managing to feed ten people three times a day. They asked for a couple of beds, a table fan, and some mosquito nets. It was the usual practice to send all such goods on a truck, but nobody was planning a trip. I asked about shipping by train but was told it wouldn't work. It would take forever to get there if at all. But I remembered the way we used to check things through on our train tickets when I was a kid in Korea and thought I'd give it a try. Two volunteers were due to go up that week. The beds were the fold-up kind. I got several yards of unbleached muslin and made sacks to cover them, stitched them shut and tied them up with plastic string. Pete and I packed up a used two-burner gas stove that was in good condition. We bought the books, tagged two bikes that could be used to good advantage, and got a big supply of peanut butter, jam, and mayonnaise. We packed and loaded all the stuff into a truck and drove to the station. With tickets in hand we were able to check it all through—no problem and no charge. It was fun. It does something to me to be told it can't be done when sometimes it can. I did learn a few things as a mish-kid in Korea.

Our newest arrival was Linda Hudak on a six-week leave of absence from her job as congressional liaison for the Department of Transportation. Her field was automobile safety, and I wish you could have seen her eyes bug out when she saw Bangkok traffic. There was no thought for safety, and we had many a good laugh at her remarks about the lack of seat belts in *tuk-tuks*—the little three-wheelers that dash in and out making an ungodly noise and filling the air with fumes.

With Linda promised to Ubon, we took the opportunity to visit the camp and accompanied her by train. The team was small and wellknit, headed by Steve Fleming, a paramedic, and his wife, Sherrill, a nurse. They were a boon to the group and at camp. After several months they took in four WYWAM (Youth With A Mission) girls who'd lost their support but wanted to extend their stay. Teaching English had some interesting challenges, and they seemed to have wisdom beyond their years.

In Asian culture parents maintain very close supervision and control of their children. Learning English is the key to freedom in their new world, and the kids picked it up in no time, easily wrapping their tongues around words that seemed impossible for adults. It gave them their own kind of liberty that threatened parental authority. Understanding that, they offered the youngsters other activities while the older population was in the classroom laboring over our difficult words and sentence structure. When the teenagers crept up to the windows to listen, they were shooed away! One of the most stabilizing factors in the midst of so much upheaval and turmoil was a strong family unit. Knowing the language before their parents threatened it. As a class broke up one day, we watched them leaving the building. Most were still working on new words, pointing to what they'd written phonetically in their own language under the pictures in their workbooks. Fully absorbed, one man walked past us saying over and over again, "Hamburger, hamburger, hamburger!"

Phanat Nikhom was a huge camp an hour's drive from Bangkok where refugees were processed for placement in countries willing to take them. We made many trips there to help those with particular needs. Most of them had checks and U.S. currency they'd received from friends and family abroad, but there was no facility for conversion to baht. Pete went to the bank and got a lot of local currency before each trip. Word spread quickly that he was the man to see. When they saw us coming through the gate, people came on the run.

He had to be very careful and made rules with which they were happy to comply. He set up shop on a table in an open-air restaurant. Only one at a time could come to him with their requests. The others had to stand back at least six feet. He knew it was risky, but he accepted personal checks as well as U.S. currency and traveler's checks. The line usually went all the way around the block, and as long as there was money they kept coming.

Some traveler's checks hadn't been signed and had to be sent back to the donor. Pete offered to send them by APO, thus making the turnaround much faster than international post and a lot cheaper. Without hesitation they gave him their checks. Their trust in Pete was touching. In all the thousands of dollars he exchanged, only one fifty-dollar check bounced. It was a risk worth taking.

One man presented Pete with a fifty-dollar bill, but Mr. Franklin's face was completely obliterated. For safekeeping, he'd worn it in his shoe while walking out of Cambodia. I asked Pete to go ahead and cash it because the serial number was clear on both sides of the note; then I asked him to buy it for me as a souvenir. I kept if for several years before exchanging it at the bank.

While Pete was playing banker, I had time to see others who had special requests.

Before we left Bangkok one day, Judy gave me the name of a family needing help. I looked them up— a young couple from Cambodia with a four-year-old son and four-month-old twin girls. The mother's milk failed, and they had used up their milk allowance from the

UNHCR. There was no baby food available, and they desperately needed money until other arrangements could be made. Judy indicated that twenty-five dollars would probably see them through.

I kept track of the money we'd received and the donors, so in the name of Paulette Landon I gave them the gift. Their gratitude was overwhelming. When I asked if I could take a picture to send to the person who made it possible, they were more than happy to oblige. They went behind a privacy blanket hung at the front of their space and dressed the girls in matching dresses they'd received from one of the agencies. Smoothing back their hair and straightening their clothes, they posed for a family picture. That night I wrote to Paulette telling her how her donation was put to use, and in the return mail she sent another gift for "her little twins."

On another trip I was asked to see a young woman named Sophia. She and her family were from Cambodia. After introducing ourselves we found a shady place to sit. She just wanted to talk and fortunately spoke flawless English. Because every refugee had a story, I coaxed her to tell hers.

"My family's from Phnom Penh," she began, "and we were very well-off. My father owned three houses. We lived in one, and the other two were rented to U.S. embassy staff. We were very happy; school was good, and we had wonderful teachers. But everything ended when Pol Pot came in. We had no idea he was such an evil man, though there were all kinds of stories about him—some good, some very bad." Her pretty face looked sad as she remembered what happened.

"It was a normal day until all of a sudden jeeps and trucks came down our street with loudspeakers blaring. They said over and over again, 'Everybody is to leave the city. Everybody out! Don't take anything with you. You can come back tonight, so just go as you are. Out, out, everybody out! No exceptions. Everybody out.'

"Trucks loaded with soldiers poured into the streets, and men carrying big guns were everywhere. They pounded on doors and demanded that we all leave right away—no hanging back or trying to hide. Anybody who didn't go would be shot. Many of them were just teenagers, carrying guns almost as big as they were. It was a terrible thing to see and so scary. We left the house and headed for the countryside—Mother and Father, two brothers, and aged grandparents who needed help. As commanded we took nothing with us.

"You probably know what happened next. When we tried to come back, they told us we couldn't after all. They wanted the city, and we could go anywhere we chose, except back to our homes. Men and boys with bayonets fixed on their rifles prodded anybody who was slow, and obviously enjoyed being so powerful. They laughed and joked and had no pity for anyone.

"That was the beginning of our slow, painful trek to Thailand. It took us many months to make our way along the 150-mile journey. My grandparents both died, and we buried them beside the road. We ate anything we could find—roots, wild berries, mushrooms, bamboo shoots—all raw and unwashed, making everybody get sick. Our stomachs ached and cramped from diarrhea, but we kept moving.

"Villages along the way were in poor condition too. Small soldiers with big guns took everything—there was no food to buy and all the shops were closed up tight. We grew very skinny, and our clothes were in tatters. From others we heard frightening stories about 'killing fields.' Having seen many guns, we knew who was doing the killing. We hid every time we saw troops on the road.

"When we finally reached the border near the Kaeodung refugee camp, the Thai guards searched us for gold or jewelry and took it away before they let us cross over. From there we were brought here for final processing.

"I'm very thankful for one good thing. In Cambodia I went to the Christian church regularly and liked it very much. I joined, but I'm the only one in my family who did. When we got here I met some of the

YWAM girls, who have explained everything to me. Now I really know I'm a Christian and very glad to have Jesus living in my heart."

"That's wonderful, Sophia," I said, "You told me you have a sponsor in Long Island, and you'll be going to the States for your senior year in high school and on to nursing training. You are a beautiful young woman, and your best years are just ahead of you."

"No," she said with a mixture of anger and sadness written on her face. "Pol Pot ate up my best years." Reaching out I took her hands in mine.

"Sophia, you are a Christian, and you can claim all the promises in the Bible, every one. In the book of Joel, chapter 2, verse 25 it says, 'I will restore unto you the years the locust ate up—the years Pol Pot ate up.' That promise is yours." She was quiet and thoughtful for a moment; it was worth the trip to Thailand to see her transformed. Tears stung her eyes and mine as a new sense of joy and release flooded her face. Her shoulders straightened.

"Yes, yes, God will give me back those years," she said.

Toward the end of October, we started thinking seriously about going home. We had no a/c in hot, humid Bangkok and only cold-water showers. The weather was a little cooler and not so damp, but being home for Christmas sounded just wonderful. We got the green light from Washington to leave at the end of November with the understanding we'd return the following March, if they needed us. Alden Lancaster, a volunteer in Songkhla, was able and willing to take over Pete's job. Anybody could do mine.

COSIGN-Washington was planning a big fund-raising drive and wanted Thai articles to sell in the Potter's House gift shop. They sent $1,000. Shopping with somebody else's money is always fun. They had a few suggestions, but I was told to use my judgment. It's a big responsibility to find things that will appeal to a wide variety of people, but the possibilities in Thailand are endless. With the last dollar spent, I packed it all up for the next homebound volunteers to take with their luggage. Sure enough, Jerry Aitken was able to get the airlines to accept it without charge. He works big magic!

Jerry and Judy went to Japan to buy surplus U.S. military goods at the Defense Department Disposal Office, DPDO. They wanted Pete to go too, but he felt he needed to stay in Bangkok to finish up his job properly. Getting that stuff was a huge bonus for COSIGN. Anything that is declared "surplus" is offered first to other government agencies, then it's up for grabs to volunteer agencies such as ours. What was left was sold off to anybody who wanted it, but most of it was of little value. The deal was that we'd pay 3 percent of sign-off value plus transportation. For example, we could buy IBM's electric typewriters for six dollars. Jerry got all kinds of things—six typewriters, twelve dental chairs, trucks, water tankers, pumps and generators—the list seemed endless, and he got it all practically as a gift. He took along a shopping list for several of the missions as well. It was all a matter of knowing how to be registered as a recognized agency that gave you a key to the candy store. After getting all the goodies, he talked a Japanese shipping company into delivering everything to Bangkok free of charge. We don't know how he did it, but that man had a golden touch and could sweet-talk people into anything.

After the goods arrived and were safely in a warehouse, Pete had his first experience in loading a ten-wheeler truck with all manner of things for shipment to Kamput on the Cambodian border. First, a two thousand-pound operating table had to be picked up at the hospital. He went over there, but nobody knew where it was. They found it on the fifth floor—no elevators—so he rounded up several men to "a-ho" it downstairs. With no loading platform, it had to be lifted from the ground to the truck bed. He told them that if anyone let go, somebody would get killed. Nobody let go. From there they went to the other side of town to load medicines, food, and huge bales of clothes until every cubic foot was filled. While coolies tied down the tarp,

Pete came home to get directions for the drivers and camp passes necessary for delivering the shipment.

"Any time I need more help, I know where to go for it," Pete said. "Those men were wonderful, cheerful, and very ready to help, and I paid them well." The workers were delighted, and the wonder of it is that Pete can't say more than a couple of words of Thai, and the coolies didn't know any English. Yet the job was done well and on time. "The next time it will be duck soup," he said. Next time? Next year we hoped.

COSIGN's largest work was at Songkhla, right on the beach, where over six thousand Vietnamese were crammed into space suitable for twelve hundred. Challenges were enormous, but our volunteers were energetic and imaginative, and the refugees were more than willing to pitch in any way they could. Family units stayed together, sometimes several to a long, thatched building up on stilts. As space got tighter, we found families living on woven mats under buildings! There were special units set aside for unaccompanied women and children and another for women who'd been raped by Thai pirates. They were a pathetic lot who received special attention from nurses and social workers.

The refugees read anything they could get their hands on, and our "library" was in constant use. The most asked for book was the Bible. At one end of the camp were two buildings side by side. One was a Buddhist temple and the other a Christian chapel. People of both faiths conducted services.

Late one afternoon I was unusually hot and tired and needed a swim. Our hotel had a nice beach where we went for a dip. There was a steep drop-off a few yards from the water's edge making the waves build up quickly to about six feet before breaking. For some dumb reason I neglected to remove my glasses, and one of the waves took them right off my face! Immediately I dived down to find them, but the rough water stirred up the coarse sand so much that it was useless. One of the first orders of business when we returned to Bangkok was to get new ones. They couldn't reproduce the trifocals on such short notice, meaning that I had to be content with bifocals.

On November 26 we headed home with a two-day stopover in Hong Kong. I love that city and wanted Pete to see it. I took him on the tram to the Peak, pointed out where we'd lived for three years, and shopped in the usual as well as unusual places. We had our Thanksgiving dinner at Jimmy's Kitchen then walked down Nathan Road. There was one glittering store after another and a dozen or more optical shops. I had the prescription for my trifocals in my purse, and on the outside chance they could fill it in twenty-four hours, we went into one. Of course they could do it, no problem. What did I expect? I gave them the frames, and off we went. It wasn't until we got back to our hotel that we realized we had absolutely no idea which shop it was! Panic time. There was nothing to do but go back the next evening and see if we could find it. I tried to recall something different about it. Just as we passed a doorway, a clerk stepped out, and calling to us he said, "Oh Mrs. Peterson, we have your glasses ready for you. Relief, blessed relief, and I was ready to pay twice the price.

Our friends met us in Los Angeles. The camper was all fixed and ready to go, as were we. Within a week we were back home, and oh my, that familiar bed felt good!

COSIGN –The Vosses

When I wrote to family and friends asking them for donations for the refugees, among the most generous were Jim and Mary Voss. They were good friends of Kedar's and mine from China days. Jim started out as a junior lawyer at the same time Kedar was fresh meat in marketing. Jim rose quickly through the ranks and ended up at the top—chairman of the board of the Caltex Oil Company. How proud we were of him!

When they received my request, Mary wrote that she'd been looking for some way to help those poor people, and here was her answer. She and Jim were about to take their last official trip around the world, visiting all the Caltex locations before he retired. When they got back they wanted to sponsor a three-generation family. They were moving to the Voss ranch in Texas and envisioned making a home for them there. The school bus stopped right at their gate for little ones, good colleges and universities weren't far away, and there was good fishing in a pond on the property for the elderly! Wow, what a vision.

On our first trip to Songkhla after our return, we met the perfect family who had just arrived from Vietnam. Tung Tran was head of household. He had elderly parents, a wife and four children, a brother, a sister and her young daughter. They had all the needs Mary envisioned, fitting the criteria so well that I didn't look further. After all, when you pray for guidance and the Lord gives it to you, you just say thanks!

Tung's English was good. I told him of Mary's request and my hope that they would be the sought-after family. He was thrilled. Everyone was looking for a sponsor in the States, and if not there, in one of the other receiving countries. At the time the United States was taking in ten thousand refugees a month!

"Tung," I said, "I'd like to take a picture of your whole family to send to Mr. and Mrs. Voss. It will help her decide if she wants to go ahead with the sponsorship program. If you'll please gather them all together I'll take one and send it to her right away." When they formed a group I could see tension and hope as they presented their best faces.

That done, they took us to a special ceremony that was about to take place down at the water's edge. To date fifty thousand refugees had already arrived from Vietnam. It was estimated that for every person who

Three-generation family

made it, one died trying. Their crafts were just fragile canal boats with a low freeboard. If they escaped detection by the coastal patrol, they encountered storms, and their little engines ran out of gas. Winds and currents swept them toward the coast of Thailand and Malaysia, and pirates attacked them before they could get to shore. Any treasures they had left were stolen; the women were raped and many killed. It was so bad that several Americans bought a small freighter in which they cruised offshore to picked up refugees and get them to safety in time. They were surely unsung heroes.

There was a special day for remembering those who died trying to make it to freedom. They built a three-foot replica of a canal boat and filled it with flowers. As they stood at the water's edge, they pushed the small craft out into the waves and prayed for the souls of the lost. I can only imagine the mixture of gratitude and sorrow they were feeling.

I began to worry when I didn't hear back from the Vosses. I sent my mother-in-law, Gertrude Bryan, Mary's phone number and asked her to call to see if she'd received my letter. While Mary and Jim were on their world tour, their ranch house was being renovated. The job was nearly completed when during the night, some flammable liquid caught fire, burning the house to the ground! As soon as they could catch their breath, Mary let me know it was still a go, and she would be in Austin the next day to fill out the necessary form. Good news!

That was another of those times I gave thanks for being the connecting point enabling something wonderful to happen. Mary and Jim rented and furnished a very nice apartment for the family in Bastrop, just a few miles from the ranch. The children were enrolled in school while the older ones got jobs and learned English. Tung was put in charge of the little country store the Vosses owned, and his wife and parents took care of the home and began adjusting to life in their new land.

Before the kids started school, Jim took them and their parents to a big department store in Austin and told them to buy everything they needed and bring him the bill! Man alive, what a blast that must have been! And he did that twice every year until they got on their feet and could manage on their own.

Tung's father was missing most of his teeth, and the ones left needed attention. With dentists so expensive, he was getting done only what he could afford. Jim heard about it.

"Tung, you take your father to the dentist, get him some new teeth, and I'll pay for them," he said. "Then old man, you and I will go to the city and chase girls!" For sure Jim hadn't changed in all the time I'd known him.

After a few years the Tran family moved to California to a large Vietnamese community where Tung worked for the state, dealing with refugees' problems. The family thrived, and once given the chance of a lifetime, excelled in whatever they did. All the children went to college, some going on to graduate school and even getting Ph.D,s.

In their generosity and kindness the Vosses have made a huge difference in the lives of those deserving people, who in turn enrich our country. We are blessed to have them.

A few years ago Jim Voss died, and last year Tung's father did. The good seed sown while they were with us has borne much fruit, and we are indeed thankful.

The youngest Tran graduates from college

Twenty years later

Yung Trinh

Tung Tran

I met the Tran family several more times, once in Phanat Nikhom, where all refugees went through processing for their final destination. Tung introduced me to Yung Trinh, the son of a close friend who had just arrived from Vietnam. He needed a sponsor, and Tung asked if I could help, too.

Yung Trinh

In 1978 Yung Trinh, who was to be an important part of our lives years later, his sister, Nga, and his older brother, Trung, made their first bid for freedom from Communist oppression in Vietnam. Months of planning, hoarding gasoline for the engine and other essentials, and huge expenditures of cash and gold for a boat all mixed in with total secrecy, ended in devastating failure when they were surrounded by dozens of heavily armed Viet Cong (VC) while they were still in the delta. Faced with overwhelming force, they surrendered.

Yung and his brother and sister were put in jail. All but their underclothing was taken away; they slept on cement floors and were fed a scoop of pig food once a day. Their frantic parents found out what had happened when Nga was allowed to go home after two months in captivity. According to custom they were permitted to take food to their sons once a month. Yung and Trung were sent to different prisons, Yung to hard labor at Chau Binh near Ben Tre, known as K-20. For sixteen months they cleared jungle for farming. They cut down huge trees with two-man saws. They had to dig up by hand deep root systems, scrape off the soil, and pile them up for burning. When all vegetation and rocks were removed, they leveled the land with hoe and shovel. Nine cubic meters a day were required of each man. It was tough, backbreaking work in the unrelenting heat, but Yung was young and strong. His skin darkened (his parents said he looked like a fisherman, which might help him escape), and his muscles bulged.

Back home again, the family planned once more for Yung's escape. For a year and a half they met daily with trusted friends, Tung Tran, and his family. Nothing was left to chance. They bought and hoarded strictly rationed gas and gave them gold to buy a boat. They studied tides and noted the dark of the moon for each coming month. Secrecy was strictly observed. Tung and Yung had a daily rendezvous. When Yung rode his bike past an alley, if Tung was there he got on the back, and they planned their escape as they rode. If Tung wasn't there, he went to their home. One morning Yung passed the alley a couple of times, and when Tung didn't show up, he investigated and found the house empty. A neighbor said they were all gone. He stood there in disbelief and growing fury at being left behind. All that planning, money, and hope were wiped out! He and his parents were devastated.

Three more times arrangements were made, but just as they were ready to go, he was warned of the presence of VC and slipped quietly away. On one attempt the cover was blown, so they scattered, trying to get away from the area. The VC set up barricades and rounded them up. All single men were told to stand together, apart from the families. Yung was holding a little girl for a friend, and because they thought he was her father, he was ordered to the family group. The single men went to prison; the families were released. Ever since then Yung has called her his angel. She's now a grown woman living in Germany.

On the last try the party of fifty-three made it safely out of the delta and were on their way. Their engine hummed along for two days then died. Left to the mercies of the currents and tides of the South China Sea and the Gulf of Thailand, they drifted. Not far from Thailand they encountered a fishing boat and for a payment of gold were towed to within a mile of Sattahip, a large Thai naval base.

They were greeted with suspicion and herded into a small, well-guarded area with no shelter or facilities and provided scant food and water. For fifteen days the Thai police questioned them and when convinced they were refugees, not VC, sent them to Phanat Nikhom.

On his first day there Yung saw Tung and confronted him.

"How could you go off and leave me?" he demanded, furious at the man who had betrayed him so cruelly.

"I was so sorry to let you down after all the planning and cost to your family," he answered. "We were waiting for you, and at the last minute we had word from a trusted friend that the VC were on their way to catch us, so I had to leave. I could not wait another minute, and there was no way I could send a message to you. Words cannot express my sorrow for you and your family, but I'm so glad that at last you have made it here safely."

Yung was slender, as they all were after years of privation, about my height, and in his early twenties.

There was an eager expectancy about him, and his bright eyes told me he was the one we were looking for. Trinity Presbyterian Church wanted to sponsor a refugee, and the young adults were eager to be involved.

"Yes," I said, "we'll sponsor Yung. I'll get right to the paperwork." Because he knew only a few words of English I gave him his first assignment.

"Yung," I said, "you'll be waiting in camp, maybe for months. It's your job to learn all the English you can—speak English; read it; think in English; sleep and dream in English!" The camp had a library of sorts, and there were daily classes. He needed to take advantage of them. I got his T (Thailand) number, full name, DOB, and all the rest so we could keep in touch.

After three months in Phanat Nikhom, he was sent to Galang, Indonesia, for six months. There he met Lenny and Mary Barklay, who were in charge of the World Relief operations in the refugee camp. Their mandate was to set up vocational guidance programs to prepare the refugees for their new lives. Several, including Yung, applied for the job of managing it. Each applicant was interviewed, several selected, and the refugees were asked to vote for their choice. Yung won by a landslide and got the job. The others were put in charge of different classes that included auto mechanics, electronics, sewing, motorcycle repair, and typing.

The first challenge was to pick out the few who could best benefit from the training. There were just forty openings and hundreds who wanted to get in. Yung found a university professor to help him write a really tough exam to get the best possible candidates and eliminate the rest. After six weeks of morning classes, new students were selected.

In the evening Yung volunteered in the Save the Children literacy program, and on weekends he established a scout troop for boys and girls. He got rope to teach knot-tying and took them out at night to study the stars, compass reading, and other survival skills. He instilled scout values and taught them games.

At the end of each week, Yung and his staff were lined up to get their pay: two dollars (twenty bhat) for Young and one dollar each for the others. He felt so rich with two dollars in his pocket. When he went to buy noodles and soup, he got chicken in his bowl too. Hot stuff and so good!

When word came that he was processed to leave, many asked why he didn't stay for a few weeks and then go, but he wasn't about to miss his chance.

The day before his departure the others gave him three parties, thanking him for all his help and kindness, and vowing to meet again in the Land of the Big PX.

He was sent back to Lumpini in Bangkok for final processing and on to Singapore before boarding the plane to Oakland, California.

On April 15, 1982, Pete and Gary and Marie Jones went to Orlando to meet him. I wasn't feeling well, and Pete had never met him. Later Yung told his side of their meeting.

"When I got off the plane," he said, "there stood Pete, holding a big sign with my name on it. He reached out his large paw that swallowed my hand and then embraced me. For the first time I heard that deep, sonorous voice. 'You are home now, Yung,' he said. All the fear and anxiety melted away that very instant. The first day of the rest of my life had been blessed beyond belief. In the words of Julian of Norwich, I knew 'all would be well and all manner of things would be well.'"

Yung arrives in the States

Yung knew what it was like to live in a modern city, but America was quite different from Saigon, particularly the one he'd left a year ago. The first time we went shopping at Publix he was amazed that there weren't clerks watching closely to see that we didn't swipe anything. It made sense to him though, when we went through the check-out line.

He needed clothes. Pete, Gary, and Marie took him shopping, and he delighted in his new slacks and jacket, saying he felt like "Little Pete." He still had a lot of English to learn, but I knew he'd pick it up quickly because that's all he heard. I remembered how it was for me in 1947 in Peking, when I learned "survival Chinese" in about three months.

Every time I was in the kitchen, he was watching at my elbow. He loved to cook and made us several wonderful Vietnamese meals. Then I watched as he chopped, minced, and did all sorts of things I never had patience for; but mmmm, it was good. While we were at it I taught him table setting, and without being asked he began to pitch in with all the household tasks.

One evening after the blessing I looked down at the table and with a horrified expression on my face, announced, "Yung, you just flunked table setting." He and Pete seemed surprised but couldn't see what was wrong.

Yung goes to live with the Webbers

"You forgot the napkins." We all had a good laugh as he got up to fetch them.

After some weeks Walt and Dee Weber offered to take him at their house, which had much more space. Their youngest, Chris, was still at home, and interaction with young people was good.

Walt was always fixing or building something at home or at Trinity, and Yung was right at his side helping, soaking up everything. His first real job was with a local marina. He was to keep the bathrooms clean and sweep the floors as needed. He went at it with a will. You can't start much lower than that, but he delighted in earning his first paycheck, $127. He didn't just stop with assigned tasks. He straightened up, picked up, and cleaned up everything that looked messy. His boss reminded him he really didn't need to do the extra work, but he felt it was better than just sitting around.

Soon after that there was a call from an "uncle" in Silver Spring, Maryland, who wanted Yung to come stay with him, promising to get him a job and into school. An *uncle* can be loosely defined as a relationship of blood or a family friend. It seemed like a good idea. Walt and Dee dropped him off there on their way north to see some of their children.

Not long after that we were in Washington visiting Mother Bryan and called him. Finding him in deep distress, we drove over to see him. There was no plan to get him into school and no job. All the uncle was interested in was making posters and banners, marching in demonstrations against the Communist government in Vietnam, and efforts to raise money to fight them.

The house had no private room for Yung. People came and went at all hours, sleeping on mats on the floor anywhere there was space. Life was chaotic. After showing us around he broke down in tears of disappointment and frustration. It was easy to see that things weren't working out as hoped. We had to get him out of there. We phoned friends at COSIGN to check on opportunities for help.

It didn't take long to learn that Tom and Julienne Baker had a commune not far away and housed several students to share costs and work. They had served with

COSIGN in Songkhla and were glad to take him in. There was space for a bed and desk in the basement next to the furnace—nice and warm in the winter and cool in the summer. They wanted him to move in right away. An answer to our prayers.

Yung had one year at the university in Saigon but no school records and had to begin all over again. He enrolled at Montgomery College nearby and immediately made a name for himself. To earn some money he took on tutoring assignments in math and French. It wasn't long until professors had him tutoring their children.

In a phone conversation, I asked Yung about his grades and which courses he was taking. All A's.

"Straight A's! That's wonderful, Yung." Later he confessed that he didn't know what I meant by "straight A's." He looked it up in the dictionary and couldn't find it. He finally figured it out. I was surprised he was taking French.

"Yung," I said, "French is one of your native languages. Why are you taking it now?"

"I need the humanities credit," he said, "and it's nice to have at least one easy course." I couldn't argue with that.

Every Christmas and summer Pete sent Yung a ticket to come to us for TLC and a wardrobe checkup. On one visit I asked about his personal life.

"Do you have a girlfriend?"

"Oh sure," he said. "There's a girl from Poland whom I help with math and a Korean I help with French."

"That's not what I'm talking about," I persisted. "Do you have anybody special you take out on dates? I know you don't have much money, so what do you do? Go out to eat or to a movie?" He looked down at his plate and fiddled with his food until Pete chimed in, "For goodness sake, Fran, leave him alone. He's a big boy now."

"I know he is," I protested, "but he's our son, and I want to be sure he's behaving himself."

"Don't worry, Fran," he said, reaching over to stroke my arm, "I'm pure." The little rascal knew exactly what I was asking and was making me work for it!

After finishing the two years at Montgomery College he came down for a visit. We drove him over to UCF to check out courses and see what was available for student housing. A Vietnamese gentleman was guidance counselor for foreign students and most helpful planning a course in math and computer science, but Yung had already been accepted at the University of Maryland, College Park, and decided to go there. He worked hard and also had a job as a teacher's assistant. The students went to the big lectures for freshman math, a required course, then met with the "TA" in classes of about thirty for further instruction.

Two students came to him saying, "Math has always been a mystery, but we must pass the course to graduate. What do we have to do to get it behind us?"

"Attend every lecture," he said. "Never miss my classes, and I can guarantee you'll make it." Yung was a born teacher. The young woman sailed through the final exam and the young man changed his major to math. Now that's teaching.

Upon graduation, Yung was inducted into the Phi Beta Kappa honor society. During the spring job fair on campus, he was courted by several major electronics companies. After checking them all out, he chose Hewlett-Packard. He said HP stood for "high price."

We couldn't make it to his graduation or later to his swearing-in ceremony when he became an American citizen. However, we were on hand at the airport in Atlanta to meet him when in June of 1987 he arrived for work. We drove him to the Picket Suites Hotel, where HP had arranged accommodations, and settled him in. My goodness, such splendor! There was a large living room/dining room, a complete kitchen stocked with basics', an enormous bedroom with a king-size bed, and a lavish bathroom. Each room had a TV, call buttons, and every kind of service you can imagine.

Yung insisted he'd sleep on the sofa bed in the living room, and we could use the bedroom, but we declined. We didn't want to get him in hot water with the company on his first day.

Pete picked him up the next morning and drove him to the HP offices. We wanted him to get on the payroll right away. I stayed at the hotel to call around to see where he could get a car.

The Presbyterian Church didn't have a member who owned a dealership, but they recommended Ed Voyles's Hyundai. It had a good reputation. That Yung didn't have any money for a down payment made leasing look like the best option.

I told agent Ken Latimer what we needed.

"We're from out of town," I said, "and are looking to lease a car for our Vietnamese son who's just starting with HP. I want to make sure we have the best possible deal and don't fancy being walked down the primrose path." That rather surprised him, but with good humor he said we need not worry. I found out he was a Presbyterian elder, which made him 100-percent okay in our books.

After lunch we drove over to the agency, found Mr. Latimer, and settled down for business.

"I've checked out everything, and I'm afraid leasing won't be possible. First of all, he's not legally your son, so you can't sign for him, and because he hasn't been with HP the required six months, they won't take responsibility for him. I suggest you buy Yung a good second-hand car." That made us blink a couple of times.

"Looks like that's the way to go," Pete said. "Do you have a good, and I mean really good, used car you can recommend?"

"As a matter of fact we do," he answered. "Just this morning we acquired one as a trade-in. It's two years old with low mileage and in excellent condition. We'll give it a more extensive check before it's released. I think we can offer it to you at a reasonable price."

"Well," Pete answered, "let's get out some sharp pencils and go to work."

We'd need a loan agreement with Yung and car insurance. I asked for the use of a desk, telephone, and typewriter (they were still in use then). It took quite a few calls to find insurance for a young man his age that wouldn't break the bank, but GEICO said yes, and I got busy working out the loan agreement.

The cost of the car, insurance for the first month, and $300.00 spending money all added up to $7,043.50. He had no money and wouldn't be paid for at least two weeks. The agreement was for twenty-four interest-free payments of $293.50 to be made within the first ten days of the month. When it was signed and notarized, I sat Yung down and gave him my five-dollar lecture on tithing. Knowing what Yung was in for, Pete sat back with an amused look on his face.

"You are a professing Christian," I said, "and it's important for you to be very careful managing your money. In time you'll have a lot of it, but it's a good idea to start tithing while you're poor. In case you're wondering what a tithe is, it's 10 percent of your gross pay.

"After you've taken care of that, put aside money for savings, probably another 10 percent; then pay your bills beginning with me. I expect to receive your check on time every month." Naturally Yung agreed—did he have a choice? We signed papers and documents, shook hands, and celebrated with a nice dinner. The car was ready to go, but there was no way we would allow him to drive it until twenty-four hours later when the insurance was operative.

We headed for home before dawn the next day. It was Mr. Latimer who picked him up and gave him the keys to his new toy.

After the loan was all paid off we gave him another to buy furniture for his condo.

Love was blooming between Yung and Rebecca Deitz, a young woman also living at the Bakers' home. They set a wedding date for August 31, 1991, in California. At that time we were due to go back to Korea to serve with OMS, but we arranged to work it into our schedule. The Vietnamese ceremony lasted all day with us participating as members of the groom's family. We were much amused when we heard Rebecca ask Yung several times, "Are we married yet?" It ended with a fabulous feast at a Chinese restaurant with many toasts to the new couple and wishes for long life, prosperity, and many sons.

The Vietnamese Wedding

The wedding in California was a formality for the benefit of the Vietnamese community and friends, so to make the union legal, they drove to Lake Tahoe, got a license, and were married in the garden of the Paradise Wedding Chapel that performs quickie marriages.

There was still another celebration for all their friends in the Washington, D.C., area at Dayspring, the retreat center of the Church of the Saviour. Yung's parents and brother from France came too.

Everything seemed to be in order when they discovered that Becky's wedding dress was missing. It was accidentally left at the house of friends with whom they were staying in Silver Spring, a good thirty-minute drive under the best of circumstances. Yung, his parents, and brother went to fetch it. When they got there Yung reached into his pocket for the key...somehow, somewhere it too was lost. There was absolutely no time to do anything but get into the house any way they could and retrieve the dress.

Yung tried every door and window on the ground floor, but they were locked up tight. Having lived there before, he thought he could get in through a window on the second floor and proceeded to climb up on the outside. People across the street saw him and called the police.

Yung told his parents that this third celebration would be quite different from the Vietnamese version, complete with music, drama, and readings. They were standing on the lawn watching him make his climb when two cars pulled up.

"Duck, duck," the police shouted at his parents and brother as they jumped out of their cars and trained their rifles on Yung. Not knowing a word of English, and thinking this was a part of the drama of the day, they stood there shaking with laughter. No matter what the police said, they just continued to laugh!

In the meantime, Yung was careful not to move, and explained his reason for breaking into the house. Very skeptical, they let him get down and warned, "If there is no wedding dress in there, the four of you will be spending the night in jail."

In no time the police had the door open, and Yung gave a huge sigh of relief, for there hung the wedding dress.

"That was a close one," the officer warned, "but if you ever need help again," he said handing Yung his card, "give me a call."

Reception in *the* dress

Ethan, their firstborn, arrived about a year later. He's a free spirit and popular with his peers. He looks like his dad, is tall and slender, and will soon tower over him.

Jordan came a couple of years later. He's of average height and of solid build. He'll probably be an engineer. He's organized, dependable, and determined.

For years the family came for a week's visit at Thanksgiving. We considered it a vacation for us too. We moved into the guestroom to make room for the whole family in our bedroom suite. We put aside most routine activities and just enjoyed being with them. When the kids were small, a trip to Disney was on the schedule, and more recently the Brevard Zoo and Kennedy Space Center were the big attractions.

At the end of one visit, Yung's departure was at 4:00 a.m. Becky's flight back home didn't come until 10:00. Pete suggested they take a room at the airport hotel, relieving concern about making their flight the next day.

"Be good to yourselves," he advised. "Swim, have dinner, and just relax the last night of your vacation." They took his advice, and got Avery! He was a cute little guy but at almost three he still wasn't talking, causing them some concern. One day when he was in his high chair, Becky left the kitchen to get something.

"Where you going, Mom?" he asked. She could hardly believe her ears. He said a whole sentence, and there was no baby talk. Right away they urged him to talk more. Once they were pointing out and naming colors. They carefully pronounced each word. They indicated another, and he said, "blue."

"He said 'blue'!"

"I'm not tupid," he answered. So he's been talking ever since and very clearly makes his wishes known. What a character! He's the thoughtful one, and often ponders things for a while before expressing an opinion. All out of the same oven are their three sons, but so different.

Thailand 1981

In the two months we had to rest and think through our next stint in Thailand, we sent out this letter of request for support for the refugees. We wrote to family and friends:

Thank you for the opportunity to tell you about our work in Thailand among the Lao, Cambodian, and Vietnamese refugees. We spent three months in Thailand in 1980 and have been asked to return in March for an additional three months. There is so much to be done (there always will be as long as there are refugees), and since the Lord has blessed us with good health, we're glad that we are free to go.

Church of the Saviour International Good Neighbors (COSIGN) is a mission of the Church of the Saviour in Washington, D.C. All who serve with COSIGN are volunteers and are provided transportation, food, and lodging.

COSIGN is assigned work in two camps: Ubon in the northeast, where most of the refugees are from Cambodia and Laos, and Songkhla in the south, near the border with Malaysia, to work with Vietnamese boat people. Other transit camps near Bangkok are visited regularly as well as several along the Cambodian border. We have volunteers living and working at both Ubon and Songkhla.

The United Nations High Commission for Refugees (UNHCR) is responsible for establishing the camps, arranging for basic food distribution, and offering minimal medical services. The Thai government is responsible for camp security. Other agencies along with the UNHCR register the refugees, search for missing family members, and assist in relocating eligible refugees in a third country. Such services would seem to cover everything necessary to care for the refugees. It is all done efficiently by professionals, but so much human need wasn't met by the system. Fortunately the "professionals" recognize it, hence the volunteer agencies have been allowed into camps to nurture these hurting people.

In Ubon the principal task is teaching survival English. Most will be resettled in English-speaking countries, and language adequacy is essential in adapting to their new homeland. Ubon is also the headquarters for cross-border feeding and assistance to several Lao villages that don't get help from any other source.

Those who came to Songkhla were from Vietnam. Except for the monsoon season that lasts about four months, the tides and currents bring them from South Vietnam to the southern coast of Thailand. Just two days before we visited the camp, eighteen refugees in a twenty-two-foot river boat landed just five hundred yards down the beach from the camp. Set upon by Thai pirates ten miles from shore, the women were raped, all valuables stolen, and their engine yanked out. Luckily the sea delivered them to us. It's estimated that only 50 percent of those leaving Vietnam ever reach friendly shores. The only kinds of craft available are canal or riverboats with little freeboard and scanty shelter. When a storm hits them, they go down. In many cases they are killed by pirates. Even with so much against them, between two to four hundred arrived every week.

In Songkhla COSIGN coordinates its work with five other volunteer agencies to teach English, crafts development, and provide special care for unaccompanied children. It operates another center for abused and raped women. COSIGN maintains all equipment in the camp, particularly the pumps for fresh-water wells that are hand-dug by our people. We have been responsible for building the post office run by a Baptist group. There are other projects to be carried out as soon as money can be raised. A well, up to 250 feet deep, is necessary to obtain clean water for the whole camp and nearby Thai village. To dig and cap the well will cost five thousand dollars. The tower, storage tanks, piping, and distribution system will take another twenty thousand dollars. A food distribution building is sorely needed to keep supplies free of rats and insects. The existing one is made of bamboo and thatch, which results in a shocking waste of food because of pests.

In the close association volunteers have with refugees, many urgent needs come to light, and insofar as is possible we try to meet them. Money for that purpose is called direct aid. For example, many are unable to read because their glasses have been lost. We can take them out of camp, have their eyes tested, and get suitable glasses if we have the money—about ten dollars. Can you imagine what a boon it would be to read again after being nearly blind for months or perhaps years? What would it be worth to you?

Buying extra food or special medicine when needed sometimes averts disaster. One such case occurred when a woman walking near the border stepped on a land mine, seriously damaging both feet. The Red Cross clinic would save her life but not her feet. A COSIGN volunteer happened to be at the clinic when she was brought in. He had money sufficient for her treatment and took her to a hospital where the necessary care was available. Both of her feet were saved.

Examples are endless but the good news is that we have people who are ready to help. Our only limitation is the amount of money we have to spend on those priceless gifts. All donations for direct aid are used for that purpose alone. Not one dime goes to overhead, so we feel free to ask you to contribute whatever you can to this cause. It will be money well spent and is tax-deductible.

If it seems right to you, and if you hear a call to help us, please make out your check to COSIGN, Inc. Send it to us or to Mr. Harold Cary, 2852 Ontario Road, N.W., Washington, D.C. 20009, and indicate that it's for Pete and Fran Peterson's work. Thank you so much.

We were humbled and touched by the response that brought in over three thousand dollars and were asked to speak in a variety of places. We visited Bonnie and Luke Staley in Charlotte, North Carolina, and during an evening social gathering met their priest at St. John Episcopal Church. He asked if we'd be willing to talk the following Sunday, and we gladly accepted, thinking it would be a Sunday School class. We arrived at the requested time and place and were handed a bulletin giving the order of worship. To our huge surprise we were listed as giving the sermon! No panic, but after a quick huddle about who would say what, we decided that Pete would go first, and I'd follow with some stories and a challenge. There were no sleepy eyes or nodding heads, and at their next budget meeting, they gave generously to COSIGN work.

When we did the same thing at Trinity Presbyterian Church, things came to us by the boxload. With our condo's storage space in short supply, the mountain began to grow in the middle of our living room, lots and lots of Bibles!

In February Dennis Bennett asked if I would give the children's sermon one Sunday. While they sat around my chair, I showed them enlarged pictures of the kids at camp.

Don't these look like nice children who would be fun to play with?" I asked. They looked carefully at the pictures and picked out kids their size and nodded "yes."

"Look carefully," I said. "Do you see boys with bikes or girls with dolls or any sort of toy?" There were none. I told them of a little girl I'd seen, holding close to her a stick wrapped in a piece of ragged cloth. It was all she had, and she pretended it was her dollie.

"I want to know if you'd be willing to share some of your old toys," I said. "We've just had Christmas, and perhaps you don't need some of last year's things. If your parents agree, perhaps you'd be willing to let Grampa Pete and me take them to Thailand for these children." They were truly excited as they scampered back to their parents.

The floodgates opened, and toys of all sorts came in from young and old alike. One woman had grandsons but no granddaughters. She wanted to make up for it by sending dolls. She'd bought several with extra outfits!

We were due to depart March 1, but I came down with a nasty sinus infection. On the doctor's advice we delayed two weeks, hoping to make the next scheduled International Committee for Immigration (ICIM) flight on the 15th. It worked out perfectly. United Airlines gave us free transportation in the States and agreed to take all fifty boxes of relief goods too. Friends showed up the morning of our departure with a trailer and got us safely on the way to our next adventure.

Fifty boxes for the refugees

Our checked baggage proved to be a problem in Oakland, however. The people at the ICIM desk said we could take just two hundred pounds apiece—the rest they'd send along when they had space, but they couldn't be responsible for it. That didn't sound very promising, but Pete had another idea. After talking to the United people, they arranged for us to have an empty ICIM container. They loaded it up with our boxes and sent it back for our flight.

As before, we arrived in Bangkok at 2:00 a.m. and thought surely the boxes would be taken to a warehouse for us to pick up the next day. But no such luck. They were the first arrivals down the chute, followed by our suitcases. As Pete grabbed them off the carousel, he called out the numbers. I checked them off the list. They were all there. Some little kids in camp would soon be very happy.

While we were organizing the shipment, an airport official strolled over. He must have had a very high rank, for he had loads of gold braid and sported a long, carved ivory cigarette holder. He took a puff then held it out to the side and used it like a pointer.

"What is all zees?" he asked.

"It's for the refugees in the camps where we work," Pete said, showing him his COSIGN identity card. We prayed he didn't want to have us open it all for inspection.

"Well then," he said with a sweeping gesture toward the exit, "get it out of here." We were ready to accommodate him right away before he changed his mind.

Same as before we weren't met, but not to worry. We knew where to go. I found a minivan big enough to carry all the stuff and off we went. This time there was a visiting pastor in our room. We unloaded all the boxes and suitcases at the house and had the taxi take us to the Rex Hotel. It was getting to be a habit.

Alden, who'd taken over the books, left sooner than expected. It meant Pete had some catching up to do with the accounts, and soon we were back in our routine of meeting new recruits and sending off volunteers, who for the most part were ready to go home but thankful for the experiences they'd had.

Home sweet home for one refugee family

Waiting for water in camp

Pete with a little one

Happy child gets a doll

Sok Son was a whole different matter. Three Cambodian villages with a total population of six thousand were located up in the mountains on their side of the border. They wanted to stay there rather than go to one of the camps, yet they needed the Thai army's protection from the Communists and support from COSIGN. Their many needs were special. They were totally dependent on outside help, and thankfully a former member of the royal family who worked in the underground was able to help us with lists. We were able to get a special kind of seed for mountain rice that needed little water, corn, and vegetables. They asked for a heavy-duty sewing machine that could stitch canvas as well as lighter materials, yard goods for clothing, and chain saws for clearing the land. Well really, they needed everything, but we tried to take care of the most urgent requests.

Armed with a fistful of direct-air money, we invaded the Bangkok wholesale industrial market to find a sewing machine and found just the right one, but it was electric and needed modification. I've done that before too. They argued that we should also get a generator, but I stuck to my guns and insisted on a belt drive and treadle stand. I won. We also bought needles for every type of use, huge industrial spools of heavy, medium and light thread for everything from tents and backpacks to blouses and baby clothes.

Next we went to the wholesale clothing market and bought basic baby and children's clothes up to age two in size. With years of poor diet and horrendous emotional stress, the women didn't get pregnant. Now that things were better and their diet improved, a huge baby boom was in progress. Jolene was with us, and together we selected girls' and boys' outfits by the dozens.

Pete made the trip to Sok Son during our first trip to Thailand; this time it was my turn. Before we left, Jerry called friends in Chantaburi about the condition of the roads. They told him there was no way to get through because the rains had begun and the roads were impassable. Jerry decided we'd go anyway. The highway was fine up to a mile and a half from the checkpoint. We'd been wondering what they were talking about until we saw the pavement end and the roadway become one wide, muddy slide. The heavy, slippery clay was so deep that the bottom of the truck dragged in it. We had a downhill start, but it wasn't possible to make it up a slight incline. We came to a complete stop. Fortunately heavy road equipment was just about five hundred yards away and not working because it was Sunday. Jerry can be very persuasive, particularly with the Thais as he knows the language so well. He took off to see what could be arranged. He was back shortly with a great big Caterpillar tractor that took us in tow and got us to the checkpoint for ten dollars. The guards hadn't received our names from the Army Supreme Command (the organization that guards all the border areas), forcing us to wait until they made contact by radio and found that we were authorized to go in. The tractor was allowed to pull us to high ground, a thousand yards beyond the gate, but then it had to leave.

The only way we could get to the base camp from the checkpoint was to ride the trailer stacked with bulgur that was pulled by a tractor belonging to the three Sok Son villages. When it was ready to go, we loaded the sewing machine, chain saws, bags of nails, and spools of wire that we'd brought on top of everything, climbed up on the pile, and away we went—very slowly. We sat at the front with our feet dangling, holding on to each other for dear life. Every now and again, the driver turned around and told us to hang on tight when we were coming to a particularly bad place. The smaller wheels of the trailer dropped into holes, nearly throwing us off. The trip was slow enough to let us have a good look at the jungle. Birds, butterflies, towering trees supported by stout vines, lacy bamboo, and mosquitoes I remember most vividly! The trip took two hours. It was a delightfully cool, overcast, most pleasant day.

We were told there was no way to take the machine up the mountain that day—everything goes up on somebody's back. I put it together and showed the camp manager how to operate it. She goes up to the villages often and would help others who wanted to use it. Jerry assembled his chain saws and taught two men to use them before we started the climb. I was given a cane, which I was certain I'd not need, but after about a thousand yards I was glad to have it. The rains had washed out most of the steps, making it slippery, and it was a job to keep going. I needed at least four hands to hold onto vines, trees, and whatever else was growing along the trail.

Fortunately though, Pete had advised me to wear my golf shoes. They helped to keep me steady. Any others would slip back about half the distance of each step. Cool day or not, we were soaked to the skin in a half hour. The streams were swollen too. There were no bridges or stepping stones, so we just waded through, looking for leeches after each crossing. We didn't pick up any. Wet shoes and socks produced some monumental blisters, but they didn't begin to bother me until the trip down. The climb was over two miles, mostly straight up.

Village street in Sok Son

As we approached the village (we visited only one of the three), we walked through a big cleared area scattered all over with trunks of large trees that couldn't be removed. The idea of the chain saws, I found, was to cut up the logs and then make them into boards for building. An attachment was available for that purpose.

The village follows the contours of the valley and is sited along a stream. It is truly a beautiful place. The houses are up on stilts about chest-high and are constructed of bamboo, palm leaves, and thatch. They are sturdy and put together with most attractive designs woven into the walls. It was free of mechanical noises; there was no pollution, and not a whiff of latrine odors. Evidently they had been very careful with sewage disposal, a small miracle in this part of the world. The one big problem was malaria. The drugs we take, cholroquin and fancidar, didn't help a bit. Only quinine was any good. We took three full doses that day, half doses three times a day upon returning, and continued them for the next ten days. We prayed we wouldn't get malaria if we were bitten. Several times I swatted mosquitoes that were feasting on me, so I took the quinine even though it made my head buzz and my ears ring.

Three of our Cambodian guides put the baby clothes in backpacks and brought them up the mountain for us. As we walked through the village, Jolene and I gave them out in suitable sizes for the babies. There was such a lot of laughter and smiles as the women accepted them. There were a dozen dresses for newborns left over—we gave them to the women with big bellies! As we were leaving, many of the mothers brought their babies out wearing the new clothes and waved good-bye.

We called in at the hospital and met the nurse who was it for all medical services. The two Australian male nurses who were there when Pete visited had gone, and one young woman fresh out of nurses' training was taking care of six thousand people! Anybody want to come and help? We took her some of the latest news, magazines and papers, and she in turn gave us lunch. We were starved and glad to sit down to rest for a while.

"Here comes the ambulance," she announced as we ate. Two men came running up the hill carrying a man in a hammock suspended from a pole that rested on their shoulders. He was another malaria victim who hadn't been able to keep anything down for three days and was running a high fever. She ordered a shot to ease the nausea, started an IV, and gave him large doses of quinine.

While we were at the hospital—a bamboo shed about fifteen by thirty feet—she showed me a little girl who had a bad head injury. One of the big eucalyptus trees fell on her, opening her skull. The large ones have very shallow root systems. When the supporting vines were cut away in clearing operations and a big wind comes up, down they go, resulting in about three accidents a week. At the time the little girl was hurt, Caroline was out of contact with the rest of the world; even her radio wasn't working. She did the best she could with a loose bandage to keep out infection, evidently the right thing as the child was doing well.

"Her grandfather carried her in a sling," Caroline said. "He never put her down. I guess that's the best kind of 'bed rest.'" Another patient had bandages all up and down his left side. It seems that during one of the frequent shellings he didn't get to the shelter fast enough, and his left arm, leg, and rib cage were peppered with shrapnel. He lived to tell about it, was sitting up in bed, and was all grins when Caroline told us what happened to him.

From the time we left the base camp until we returned in the evening, we were escorted by several Cambodians carrying M-16s. One time we heard some distant shooting.

"I hope somebody got a rabbit for dinner!" Jerry remarked.

Our return from the base camp to the checkpoint was rough. This time we had to sit sideways on a load of bamboo strips being sent out to market, with our feet stuck out in front of us. We had to hang on to a big frame on the side. By the end of two hours, I thought my back would never be the same. Jolene and I put a pad out in the back of the pickup and slept most of the way to Bangkok. We were so sore and tired that nothing could keep us awake. We got home at 2:30 a.m., showered, and just died for the rest of the night. It took me two days to recover, but I wouldn't have missed it for anything. It was truly high adventure.

The tractor that pulled people and supplies back and forth is the only contact those three villages have with the rest of the world. I noticed that one of the tires was in very poor condition. It had a big patch bolted on. I asked Lane, the village chief, if there was any plan to replace it. He said he'd asked several organizations to help, but so far he had no reply. About six thousand villagers depend on that tractor, so it seemed a good thing to help. It cost $350 for one tire, and would you believe it, a couple involved in earth-moving equipment gave us just exactly that amount! We could give it because so many have given to us. Again, thank you!

Thailand 1981 Twan

"Help!" came the urgent call from Chet, the COSIGN director in Songkhla, "Please see what you can do about getting Twan cleared for refugee status in the States. He's been moved to Bangkok and absolutely refuses to go to Australia. We're afraid he'll be in big trouble if he keeps bucking the system."

Twan, one of the brightest and best refugees from Vietnam, indeed had a problem. He wanted to go to the States, but the UNHCR insisted he could not because his relatives were in Australia. He must go there too.

His is an interesting but sad story. He's a tall, good-looking young man with flawless English. He made himself useful at the camp helping COSIGNers dig wells, and everybody liked him. The camp was located right on the beach, so the water was brackish but suitable for bathing and laundry. Drinking water was delivered in tanker trucks.

On Sundays they didn't work, and unless there was an emergency, COSIGN volunteers stayed at the residence a couple of miles away. It was terribly hot, although there was a rest period for a couple of hours in the middle of every day, they were glad for the break to read, do their laundry, and write letters.

One Sunday Twan and his friends decided to keep working on a partly finished well, even though the supervisor wasn't there. One man was down at the bottom filling the bucket with sand, and the others were on the surface hauling and dumping it. The work was going well.

A young boy came to see what was going on and went right up to the edge to have a look. As he left, his foot turned on the rim, loosening the sand, and the whole side caved in. Twan's best friend was buried under tons of sand!

They dug frantically with hands and shovels, but it was too late. When they finally reached him he was dead and couldn't be revived. Twan was devastated. When word came the next day that he was cleared to depart for the States, he turned it down because he needed to bury and mourn his friend. His space was given to the next in line. Three months later, another notice came that he was cleared again, but once more he refused because he wanted to secure a marker for the grave.

Twan applied once more, but in the interim a cousin in another camp and his family accepted haven in Australia. According to UNHCR rules, Twan had to go there, too, and entry to America was no longer possible.

There seemed to be no justice. According to custom, Twan had done the right thing for his friend. He was being denied his dream of living in the States, and we were denied a good citizen.

Everybody did what he could. We wrote letters, made phone calls, and went to the U.S. embassy to plead his case, but nothing worked—the UNHCR's rules were law, and that was final.

Twan was moved to Lumpini transit camp just two blocks from the embassy in the heart of Bangkok, still fighting for a chance to emigrate to the States.

We were scheduled to depart for home the next day. There was nothing to do but go to the embassy and try one more time. Pete was busy balancing the books; it was up to me.

The consular officer heard me out, called UNHCR for Twan's file; then we waited and waited and waited. After two hours it was determined that the file was "lost" in transit. It was clear that they had no intention of helping. I thanked them and walked to Lumpini, showed my pass to the guard, and went to the Vietnamese section.

My job was to spell out very clearly what his options were and talk him into accepting refugee status in Australia. He was stubborn, and I wondered if he'd listen. While I spoke, he never looked me in the eye. Standing tall right in front of me, hands clasped behind his back, he looked at his feet. He didn't nod or give any indication that he was listening.

"Twan," I said, "all of us have done everything possible to get you cleared for the States, but we're blocked because your uncle and his family have gone to Australia. The UNHCR rule is clear. They won't change their minds no matter what we do or say. You know how much we like you, Twan, and we want every good thing for you, but I must tell you now, your best bet is to accept Australia's invitation." Twan gave no response, so I kept going.

"Pete and I are leaving tomorrow, and this is our last chance to help you. I was told today that if you refuse to go to Australia, they have no choice but send you to C-Q, and you know about that place, don't you?"

Nothing.

"It's where they send all the bad people who come in with the good refugees—murderers, robbers, and troublemakers. If you go there you'll be imprisoned for a long, long time, and maybe when you're an old man they'll ship you back to Vietnam. You don't want to go there, Twan."

Nothing.

"Australia is very kind to their refugees. They'll give you a place to live and help you get a job. You'll do well there, Twan, and in time there is no reason you can't go to the States. The relations between our countries are very good."

Nothing.

"Twan," I said in desperation, "what will you do?"

"I will obey you," he declared, jerking his head up and looking me in the eye.

I took a step toward him, and we embraced. I didn't know whether to laugh or cry. I was so thankful that he was able to bend a little and accept this new opportunity for his future. He will have a good life.

I don't remember the trip back to the COSIGN house. I must have floated. Once more I was happy at being in a position to help.

Pete closed the books; we packed and were ready for the next adventure.

Fran L. Peterson

Home Again 1981
Going Space-A

On June 28 after a lot of hugs, kisses, and best wishes from the Aitken family, Jerry drove us to the airport where our passports were stamped. We then boarded a bus out to the tarmac where the U.S. Air Force C-130 was loading. Talk about hot—it was like an oven in the huge, empty plane. They had just unloaded cargo and were returning to Clark AFB in the Philippines. A few seats were there for the ones making the trip, but it definitely was not a passenger flight. We bought packed lunches and drinks, and the only "facility" was halfway up the sloping hold, completely open and without a courtesy curtain. We departed at 11:30 a.m. for a seven-hour prop-job flight. As soon as we were airborne, the a/c kicked in, which was a blessing, but the noise was deafening, and we understood why earplugs were issued. We used them.

It was our first experience flying military space-available, and we soon found it can be a challenge. The cost was ten dollars apiece; our only travel expense. That's my kind of deal.

Going through customs at Clark, we were told to move through the line, where the inspector would open every fifth suitcase. Wouldn't you know that mine was number five. I reached over to unlatch it when the man behind the counter stepped back with a look of shock and surprise on his face.

"I can't believe this," he sputtered. "You're a dead ringer for my aunt. I'll swear, you look exactly like her. Go on, go on through. I'll get the next bag." I moved along and he went through Pete's.

Surprising as this was, it was not unusual. I've been told by dozens of people that I look just like someone they know. When we were living in Leonia, New Jersey, in 1954, the New York subway system had a poster in their cars urging one and all to attend their place of worship. There was a picture of a man and woman sitting in a pew with a couple of children, and the woman could have been my twin.

The BOQ (bachelor officers' quarters) at Clark were wonderful. In Chambers Hall we had a beautifully furnished room and private bath. Such luxury, and at eight dollars a night we were ready to stay forever. I had no idea we were so tired, but with no plans for a couple of days, we slept late, napped, and went to bed early.

With a letter from the U.S. embassy in Bangkok in hand asking that we be permitted to check out any and all Defense Property Disposal Office (DPDO) for items of benefit to the refugees, we were taken to Clark's facility and the one at Cubic. Pete looked around for things on the wish list, and as he found them I wrote them down, but there wasn't much.

After checking on flights to Korea for a few days, we got the last two seats on a medivac plane to Koon Son. The plane was going on to Osan, where we really wanted to go. When we were airborne and the flight nurse came by to ask if there was anything she could do for us, Pete asked if we could stay on the plane to Osan. In five minutes she returned saying that of course we could. That got us much closer to Seoul—just a two-hour bus ride, and they left every half hour.

The Neija Hotel was a Rest and Recreation (R&R) military facility, whose rates were all of twenty-seven dollars a night for both of us—a little more than the eight dollars at Clark, but still a gift. We checked in for a week and the next day contacted a number of folks I'd known since I was a kid.

Everything had changed dramatically since our evacuation in 1950. There were only a few places that looked familiar—the train station, the north and south gates, and the original quadrangle at Younsei University. During the Korean War, Seoul changed hands six times, and with all the shelling was in a shambles. Huge modern buildings rose from the ashes, making it truly a Phoenix city. In 1940 there was one bridge over the Han River to the fields and small villages on the other side. Now there were eighteen. High-rise apartments and commercial buildings fifteen to twenty stories high gobbled up more and more land. Subways and super highways kept people on the move, and the air of expectancy and energy was real.

We took a day to check out the DPDO at Camp Market, where the opportunities were better. We sent off a long list to Jerry for his consideration.

On July 16th, we were back at Osan to catch a flight to Japan, and there were plenty of seats on the contract carrier. We were still traveling on our initial charge of ten dollars!

After a couple of days in Tokyo, we returned to Yukota to try for a flight to Hawaii. During the day we stuck pretty close to the terminal to be on hand for scheduled as well as nonscheduled flights. We were well fortified with good books and a couple of decks of cards. The VIP lounge was nice, and there were others with whom we shared many hours of bridge while taking advantage of complimentary coffee and snacks. Getting out of Japan wasn't easy unless you wanted to go to Diego Garcia, and flights to Hawaii weren't showing up at all. Two or three at a time, others going space-a gave up and went home on commercial flights, but we were determined to hang in there a little longer.

On the 18th we met Colonel Keating from Hawaii and asked him if he had a suggestion on how to get there.

"Well," he said, "I just came in on a C-141 resupply plane that will be returning empty tomorrow. I'll see what I can do about getting a few seats put in there." That was such good news, though whether he'd acutally be able to do it was a question.

We went to the terminal on the 21st at 6:00 a.m. to be on hand for all flights. Still nothing to Hawaii, so we had breakfast at the snack bar. Pete stayed to monitor flights, and I took a big bag of dirty clothes to a BOQ laundry three blocks away. I had two machines going great guns when Pete came in, panting.

"There's a plane to Hawaii in a half hour. Hurry! I'll check us through customs and passport inspection, and we'll be on our way." I put both machines on "spin," got out as much water as possible, then stuffed the wet, soapy clothes in a couple of plastic bags and joined Pete just as the line was beginning to move. It was too close for comfort.

We landed at 1:00 a.m. and got a room at the Hale Koa R&R hotel. It was wonderful to be on home soil again and see the American flag flying everywhere, always a beautiful sight.

We called on friends and did tourist things such as visiting the *Arizona* Memorial. After that we were ready to make the last run for home. We began to check flights to the States. On the 24th we went to the terminal at Hickham. There we found some nice sofas to stretch out on in the VIP lounge to be on hand at 6:00 the next morning.

The first flights to the West Coast were full, but a nonscheduled flight to Tyson, Tennessee (Knoxville), was announced. There were two no-shows, so guess who got the seats! It was a tanker plane operated by the Tennessee National Guard on their way home after six weeks of deployment. The crew had commercial airline seats and several bunks, and we passengers had bucket seats all around the sides and were provided with masks and small bottles of oxygen in case we lost pressure.

Once we were airborne the load master came back to instruct us about safety measures and what to do if we had to ditch. He was a great big man, about six feet four inches, and looking up at the ceiling, he concluded his remarks with: "Now you know, folks, we're busy up here on the flight deck, so we don't want any of you comin' up here for a visit. I don't keer if you're a gen'ril; we don't want you." We sure enough got the word.

Within the first half hour, one of the crew came to ask if I'd like to take one of their extra seats. Of course I said I'd be delighted. Not five minutes later they asked Pete, too.   On all our space-a flights we were given every courteous attention, making me appreciate more than ever Pete's rank of colonel.

We had trailer accommodations that night, and thus ended our travel—all the way from Thailand on ten dollars each. Our flight back to Florida cost ninety-nine dollars.

Haiti

In June of both 1983 and 1984 we joined the Young Life group from Orlando under the direction of Charley Scott on a work mission to Haiti. There's a little independent Baptist church in Pele, one of the worst slums of Port-au-Prince. When asked what they needed most, they begged for a school. Illiteracy is about 85 percent, which leaves them in abject poverty. More than a medical clinic they wanted education for their children.

Building materials were locally available, but we had to help raise money to cover the cost. We took food for our group and toys and clothes for the children.

A fifteen-foot-high cinder-block wall surrounded the L-shaped, one-acre compound with the sanctuary in the short section and the school buildings lined up on the long side. The open area was to be used for a playing field, but at the time it was full of construction materials.

We understood we'd be sleeping in the church, but after one look we changed locations in a hurry. It was filthy; the floor was covered with dirt, and bugs were everywhere. Never in my life have I seen such huge cockroaches. They had to be at least three inches long. The flat roof of the five-room administration building under construction still had rebar sticking up, but there was plenty of room between them to accommodate our bedrolls. One of the kids found a bamboo ladder, and up we went. Perfect. After the sun went down it was cool; there was a nice breeze, and it was clean. We had only one night when it rained, but by then we'd swept and washed the floors in the sanctuary, painted the walls inside and out, and sprayed thoroughly with Dursban. The creepy-crawlies don't like that stuff! The benches weren't attached to the floor, so we moved them around in pairs facing each other to make sleeping platforms. Ceiling fans made it tolerable.

The community toilet was a challenge. Located in the far corner of the compound behind the church was a pit covered by two boxes with holes in the center. The smell was enough to shut down your elimination for at least three days. But it was all we had, and was it dirty! Everybody used it, including two hundred school children. They had no toilet paper, so hands were used and then wiped on the walls. First thing every morning I filled a bucket with water, added a big slug of Pinesol, and washed everything down. Then I called our gang to go while it was still clean. We had paper. Before we left, one of the men painted the seats, making cleanup much easier.

During our stay, four of the five rooms of the administration building were completed. Workers leveled the earth, spread gravel, and poured the concrete floors. The Haitian crew inserted the reinforced corner posts and built up the cinder-block walls to the height of the second floor. All of the work was done by hand. The men hauled water, sand, and gravel by the hour. Adding water to the cement a few gallons at a time, they mixed with shovels until the boss man said it was just right. They loaded it into a wheelbarrow, pushed it to the area being worked on, dumped it, and spread it out. That was hot, hard work, but all the guys, including Pete, stuck at it for hours at a time in the most unbelievable heat. Some of the girls hauled water, and even tried to mix cement, but that didn't last long. They did all the laundry by hand, without the benefit of even a scrub board and with a severely limited water supply. They did a good job, and I heard not a word of complaint.

Water from the city came on every other day for a few hours in a single outdoor tap. As soon as it started everyone filled buckets and basins then directed the flow into a large cistern. The tap water was okay for laundry and bathing, but not for drinking and cooking. We got five-gallon bottles of Culligan for that. Cistern water was full of all manner of livestock, okay for mixing cement, but when we had to use it for cleaning fruit or washing dishes, we added a lot of germicide, thanks to Paul and Ona Shupe of AMWAY.

After such hard, hot work a late afternoon shower felt wonderful. The one and only stall was located outdoors, attached to the end of the administration building. A pipe ran from the fifty-five-gallon drum atop the building and through the tin roof of the stall. At the pipe's end was a showerhead that could be turned on and off. A dark blue plastic curtain provided privacy. Water had to be carried across the yard from the tap and up the ladder then dumped into the drum. Every drop was precious, and it was nice and warm from the sun. The deal was to run just enough water to wet the washrag, turn it off, soap up and scrub, then turn the water back on and rinse off as quickly as possible. Average use was about a half gallon each. The girls used more when they washed their hair.

At first there was no drain, and we had to stand ankle-deep in other people's stagnant dirty water. Pete and Charley Scott put in some cinder blocks to stand on, but it was still disgusting because the water looked awful and smelled worse. I talked them into opening up a drain hole through the wall, which worked just fine. I tell you, it was really "uptown." The next work group following ours had no idea how well off they were. Before we arrived for the second year, a flush toilet was installed in one of the new buildings. Oh joy! There was still a water shortage, so I posted a little poem we'd used in Hong Kong.

> If it's yellow, let it mellow.
> If it's brown, flush it down.

Life gets real.

Each of us was paired with a Haitian from the church. Working or free time we spent with our partners. After breakfast we had worship in both English and Creole. They taught us choruses in their language, and we taught them ours. At midmorning and midafternoon breaktimes, we had a drink and played games or rested. Charley brought a basketball hoop, which he hung up the first day, and a ball. It afforded much competition. In the evening after supper we played card games, told stories, and had another time of worship. It wasn't long before we were able to converse in a mixture of both languages.

Probably the best part of the whole experience was to see the beautiful faith of our Haitian counterparts. They know their Bible and have committed long passages to memory. It's an inspiration to hear them pray. Most of them began with *Cher Papa*. (Dear Daddy). Their prayers were simple, direct conversations with the Father, and they were beautiful.

The two of us with Pete's partner

On our first Sunday, my partner, Joseph Ives, asked Pete and me to come to his house to pray for his mother. She had a heart condition and could rarely get out of the house. We understood they lived just a short distance from the church, but we got there only after walking two and a half miles through the worst slum I have ever seen—and oh, the smells! The tiny house was as neat as a pin, and the little woman was a dear. Every other sentence she said, *"Preyer Senur."* (Praise the Lord.) We read some scripture, prayed for her, and left when it was time to go back for supper. It was so hot we were soaked to the skin, and the stench was beyond description. But as I look back on our time in Haiti, it was one of the best parts of our stay.

Several times we took trips out of the compound. We walked the streets of Pele to see what it was like. Talk about poverty; we were in its capital. The dirt "streets" were about four feet wide with open sewers on both sides. Houses were packed close together and made mostly of scrap lumber or whatever else was could be found. There was no flooring, and when there was a hard rain they flooded. Reluctant to leave their homes, parents had to sit up or stand, holding their young all night so they wouldn't drown. Can you imagine living like that?

One afternoon we went to the beach for a swim, but our best outing was a trip up the mountain to visit the Baptist mission. Even in the middle of the day it was cool, cool, cool. What a relief! Fresh garden vegetables were available, and they ran a very nice souvenir shop.

Within a day of our arrival, the woman who was responsible for cooking for the gang said she couldn't cope, so I offered to help. That evolved into my doing the whole thing. Not to worry; you do what you can with what you have, and it works out. Daily shopping was necessary because our only refrigeration was a large portable cooler. The "kitchen" consisted of a table and a two-burner bottled gas stove. One ring was about six inches wide, the other about the width of your thumb— just big enough to keep the coffee hot. It was challenging to cook for forty people, but they ate in relays.

We brought lots of peanut butter, margarine, and Velveeta with us. Jam, bread, the best ground beef in the world, and fruit were locally available. I made syrup from brown sugar and water. When it was done, adding margarine and Haiti's wonderful vanilla made it super. I rotated three breakfast menus: pancakes, French toast or scrambled eggs, coffee, and fruit. Each evening I gave money to one of the women of the church to buy the fruit first thing in the morning. Three times a day we had wonderful mangoes and bananas. Lunch was usually some sort of sandwich or burger, chips, and fruit along with soft drinks. I tried to have a hot meal such as spaghetti every night, drinks, and fruit. The last day I gave them their favorite meal of grilled cheese sandwiches, applesauce, and peanuts. Try that some time, not bad. We all worked so hard all day that we were hungry for anything. It was good.

The little children of the neighborhood came into the compound to play with our kids. When they weren't busy with the building, our workers made a big point of giving the youngsters a lot of attention. There was much hand holding, and the little ones weren't all that clean. When I was ready to serve food, I called out, "Everybody wash hands, hold them up over your heads, and come eat." I'm sure that helped keep us healthy.

One of the smallest kids was about two. He came buck-naked and had a huge belly, probably from roundworms. I got out little shorts and a shirt and put them on him, but every night he returned, still naked. After the fourth evening I ran out of clothes that fit him.

He was a darling little guy. Every time I sat down to eat, he came and stood right in front of me. I quickly ate what I needed and fed him the rest. He stood there, never taking his eyes off mine, opening his mouth like a little bird, holding on to his earlobes.

Many of the children had raw spots on their faces, arms, and legs. They didn't look infected or runny, but there was no skin! They varied from pin-head size to patches as large as a quarter. I found a first-aid kit containing alcohol, cotton balls, iodine, lots of Bactroban cream, and hundreds of Band-Aids, which I put to good use. That did the trick. The spots disappeared in a couple of days. And they loved the Band-Aids! There were so many to treat, and they crowded so close that they were right on top of me. Pete lined them up to give me a little room. One little guy, the grubbiest in the compound, had spots on his chin and forehead. He also had a big belly and runny nose, typical of children with roundworms. I got him to sit still long enough to wipe his nose and treat his spots. Man alive, did he ever feel like hot stuff when we put the Band-Aids on his face! He came back every day for more, and we kept him adorned even when the spots were gone. Why not? Such a little thing to make him happy.

An older boy came to me late one evening with a bad cut. Somehow, he had sliced off the top of his little toe, nail and all, and a part of the side. It was hanging by a flap, and was full of dirt. I had Pete hold his foot while I washed it with drinking water, dried it, then cut off the flap with my nail clippers! No, they weren't sterilized. After dressing it, Pete got some of his socks and tennis shoes for the lad. The day we left he showed me his foot. It was completely healed!

I never worked harder or felt better.

On our last Sunday, there was the usual two-hour service in the morning. In the evening, they put on a three-and-a-quarter-hour service especially for us. Sitting on those hard benches and in that heat it seemed even longer. But I loved the last part when they enacted a morality play. The story was about a minister who got hooked on gambling and lost everything. He was down and out, but his Christian community comforted and restored him. The fun was seeing the reaction of the congregation. They cheered and clapped for the good guys and hooted the bad ones. The little kids were having the time of their lives. It was great just watching them. They crept closer and closer to the platform—climbing right up on it until they were shooed off. There was no radio or TV, and most shacks had no electricity. Going to church and having a play, too, was big-time entertainment.

At the end of our mission in 1983 several of our Trinity kids, Chris Weber, Scott Mock, Peter Varcoe, and Ellen Armestad said they would never go to Haiti again, but in early 1984 when we let it be known that we were planning another trip, guess who were first to sign up.

Taipei, Taiwan
IESC

Taipei was unbelievably hot that August Sunday in 1985. We'd arrived from the States the night before determined to take full advantage of every day of our three-month stay.

While meeting congregants at the end of the worship service at the International Protestant Church, we were invited to teach conversational English to university students and young professionals on Wednesday nights at ORTV, a Christian broadcasting company. No preparation was necessary; we just had to show up at the specified time. We'd be told about the lesson and provided with a few guidelines. The rest was up to us. Wow, what a challenge! We said we'd think it over and let them know.

Pete and I were in Taiwan at the invitation of the International Executive Service Corps (IESC) to help the Sun Moon Star Company sort out their

118

manufacturing problems. Soon after WW II, people with a lifetime of experience were invited to share their know-how with struggling establishments in third-world countries. It was a joint effort by our government and that of the inviting nation. The expert and spouse were invited to come for up to ninety days. Their way would be paid. They also provided a stipend in U.S. dollars to cover all expenses.

Pete was picked up from our hotel at 7:00 each morning, driven out to the factory some twenty miles away, and delivered back at around 6:00. It was a long day for him.

The Marble Factory

Marble, marble everywhere in green, gray, and white; on hotel lobby walls and floors, in posh offices and homes, and in all manner of carvings from enormous dragons, elephants, and decorative fountains, to lamps, bracelets, and rings!

A spine of high mountains runs the length of Taiwan. Soon after Chiang Kai-Shek moved his government to the island from mainland China, it was apparent that he needed to have better contact between the two sides. There were improved roads, but the mountains were high and steep and not suitable for

119

military traffic. Constructing a new highway through the Taroko Gorge was a priority.

It was a long, tedious process with high loss of life. While blasting out the rock, enormous deposits of marble were discovered, giving rise to a new industry. One of Taiwan's tourist attractions is a visit to the gorge to learn all about how the highway was built. Naturally, at the end of the day there was an opportunity to buy whatever took your fancy. We signed up for a two-day weekend trip.

As Pete and I waited for the train to arrive, an amusing scene unfolded a few yards away. An elderly man squatted at the edge of the platform next to the empty tracks with a small boy sheltered between his legs. We soon learned why. A beautiful arch of golden rain sparkled in the early morning sun as the child relieved himself. We smiled. It was so normal, so Chinese.

The train trip took most of the morning; then after lunch we boarded buses to travel the Taroko Gorge highway. There were many tunnels and spectacular views of the mountains and valleys from the cliff-hanging highway. Every turn in the road presented a new vista. It reminded us a little of the highway across Canada along the Columbia River.

Before dinner we went to the factory, where huge slabs of marble were cut into blocks for industrial use and on to see how the carving was done on decorative pieces. Large, noisy power tools did the rough sculpting, but as details were cut and polished, the drills got smaller and smaller. Although there were standard pieces that appeared to be mass produced, every one followed a master design and was individually carved. Next stop: showroom and sales pitch.

I've always liked the Chinese lions that are standard fixtures guarding temple gates, palaces, and homes of the wealthy. They are male and female. The way you tell them apart is that the male lion has his right paw resting on a globe, and the female has her left paw holding down her cub on its back—with her claws in its mouth!

Thinking it would be a nice gift for our children at Christmas, I picked out a pair of white ones and asked the clerk how much they cost.

"Two hundred fifty dollars," she announced without blinking an eye. "That includes packing and shipping to the States. Insurance too," she added quickly.

"No, no," I answered, "I can't possibly pay so much. Can you come down?"

"Oh, this number-one best marble," she informed me, "very rare, and hand-carved too."

"I know," I agreed, "it's beautiful, but you've a whole mountain of the stone, and it's all carved by machine. We just saw it next door. How much can you come down?"

"Just for you," she whispered, "two hundred dollars. That's a good price," she said with a wink. By this time Pete knew he needed to absent himself. He didn't like to bargain. If he wanted something he bought it, but bargaining is in my blood as it is for the Chinese. We love to go at it, and I was just getting warmed up.

"How much you pay?" she asked.

"One hundred dollars," I said with a straight face.

"Oh my, oh my, no can," she answered, horrified, but she wasn't ready to give up yet. "Why not two hundred? It really good price for such fine marble—the best we have."

"No, sorry, one hundred is my last offer." She made a pouting face and continued to point out the merits of "the best pair in the house," but I wouldn't relent. For one hundred it would be worth it, but not a penny more.

"You wait," she said. "I get my boss and see what she say." They returned smiling broadly, carrying a tray of tea. I was offered a cup and enjoyed the fragrance of the jasmine brew.

The manager congratulated me on my selection.

"How about two hundred," she said, holding up two fingers. I reached over, folding down one finger.

"How about one hundred?"

"Okay," she said. "You drive a hard bargain, but okay. You can have them for one hundred dollars." I really didn't think they would meet my offer, but once they did I was stuck with it. There was just one problem. At forty pounds each, they were heavy little suckers. Now we had to get them home. Not to worry. We'd figure out something. The factory delivered them to our hotel room. First step completed.

That evening we were treated to a delicious Chinese feast followed by a program of music and dance by an aboriginal tribe. The next morning we went to the train by taxi, and this time the tour guide managed the lions. He put them at our feet on the train, and when we reached Taipei, he carried them to the taxi that delivered us to the President Hotel. The doorman took them up to our room. All that cost some heavy tipping, but it was worth it.

During our stay in Taiwan I collected a variety of things for my friend, Jill Moyer, who imported Asian artifacts. She agreed to let me send the lions in her shipment. When the buying was all done, the hotel bellhop took the lions from our room to the taxi, and the clerk at the shop where the shipment was being assembled carried them into the store.

While Pete was at work, I was free to enjoy exploring the city, meeting various interest groups, and shopping. Pirated books were dirt cheap, and I indulged in a reading feast. When the second Wednesday rolled around, we decided to try the ORTV thing on for size. We could at least go once, we reasoned; if it wasn't our cup of tea we'd excuse ourselves. But we were hooked.

In the premeeting session we went over the Bible text and were offered several suggestions, but with the reminder that they'd come to practice and hear English. If the conversation wandered off course, it was okay. Just let it flow wherever it would.

Around two hundred came each time, filling the hall with the happy buzz of many voices. After a few opening remarks, someone read the text in Chinese then English, each student following carefully in the *Good News for Modern Man* translation of the Bible. After a quick lesson the teachers made their way to meeting areas throughout the building; students went wherever they chose.

We met on the stage with about twelve. A core group of five returned to us each week. Others stayed for a class or two and moved on. After a short discussion, we asked questions, but if anyone decided to pass, that was his option. Each took a biblical name. Thomas never asked a question. He always passed. In our second month, he spoke up for the first time.

"I want to say something."

"Of course, Thomas," Pete said.

"When I come here," he began, "I must to buy this book. At first it is just many pages and many words, but now when I read it, the words burn in my heart."

Wow, I thought. He's not a Christian, but the scriptures are having an impact on some area of his life. From then on Pete and I prayed particularly for Thomas. During our last meeting at ORTV, once again Thomas announced that he had something to say.

"Yes, Thomas," Pete encouraged, "we are eager to hear you." Slowly, hesitantly, he shared a family problem with the class.

"When I first meet with my girlfriend she always late, always. I not care too much; I love her and she love me. One year our parents agree, and we marry. Now we have two children. I go to my job and she work for a lawyer, but she still always late. It make me so angry. Sometimes I want to hit her, and that very bad.

"Last night I wait for her in our car, and as I sit there I get more and more angry, hot and mad, until I remember what I read in this book. Slowly I became very calm and quiet. When she finally come, I can greet her. I'm okay. I think Mr. James write a good book."

"O Lord," I breathed in prayer, "Thomas is so close. So close. Don't let him slip away now." As we waited for a taxi to take us back to the hotel, Thomas stood with us. I took both his hands in mine.

125

"Thomas," I said, "we are so sorry to be leaving you just now, but we know God has his hand on you. Be sure to come back here every week and find a church where you can worship and learn more from this wonderful book." Tears hung on his lashes as he nodded. The taxi came; we waved good-bye to the other students and left.

Back home in Florida during the Christmas season, we received cards from our ORTV students, but we will always cherish the one from Thomas. It was a cheap commercial greeting, but his words transformed it into a treasure. "Thanks to you, my good teachers, me know God."

In early December the Moyers received the shipment containing our lions. We drove to Bonnie (Pete's daughter) and Luke Staley's for Christmas in Carmel, Indiana, and the Moyers were going to Florida at the same time. We arranged to meet for lunch where our paths crossed in Pennsylvania, and transferred the lions from their car to ours. At last they appeared under the tree on December 25, 1985.

To Shalom House

On November 15, 1985, we said our good-byes and boarded the plane for Seoul.

For months before leaving the States we had let it be known that we were available to serve. One possibility that interested us was the United Mission to Nepal Guest House in Katmandu. It was a joint effort of Protestant missions to accommodate those who came there to work for several months or just to visit for a few days. With our experience in Thailand, we thought we would be qualified to handle such a job.

While we were still in Taiwan a letter arrived from Eileen Moffett, a missionary friend in Korea, asking if we'd be interested in the Shalom House job. You bet! Since we were already in the "neighborhood," we thought we'd take a quick trip over there on our way home, and check it out. At Eileen's suggestion, I wrote to Don and Julie Sansom, directors of Shalom House, asking if there was any way we might be of service to the center if and when they went on leave. We didn't hear from them until we were in Taiwan, where we received a letter forwarded to us from home. In it Don said that they planned to go on leave for six months starting in September 1986 and wondered if we were still available

It took just three hours to fly from Taiwan to Korea, and we checked in at the Neija, a military R&R hotel. We went from the tropics to the first cold snap of the year in Seoul. I had my London Fog, but Pete had just his suit, and nearly perished until we could get to I'Teawan to buy him a down-filled jacket.

At church the next day, we met several missionaries I had known as a child in Korea, among them Carol and Dick Underwood. It was like old home week. After lunch, Kem Spencer, another missionary, drove us up to visit Shalom House, which was just outside Camp Casey, headquarters for the 2nd Division that mans the demilitarized zone (DMZ) between North and South Korea.

Kem served on the board of Shalom House and was enthusiastic about the prospects of an arrangement that would allow us to fill in for the Sansoms during their absence.

It all seemed providential because their regular board meeting was scheduled for the following Tuesday

128

at 2:00 p.m. Pete and I caught the 9:00 a.m. military bus from Seoul to Camp Casey. Because Pete is retired military, we got all sorts of perks that made it easy for us to function in Korea. We had the morning at Shalom House with the Sansoms and a tour around the several bases nearby before the board members arrived for the luncheon meeting.

By this time we could clearly see that Pete's gifts of management and mine of hospitality fit with their needs, so when they asked if we'd be willing to come, we said yes. That gave them enough lead time to arrange visas, which were more and more difficult to obtain, and so "if the Lord was willin' and the creek didn't rise," we'd be leaving home around the middle of August for overlap time with them at Shalom House before they departed on the first of September. It was exciting, and we looked forward to the experience with great anticipation.

We had instructions on how the House was run and what would be required of us. It was a busy place. There was a school, K through eight for children of servicemen, most of whom had Korean wives. An assignment to Camp Casey is an unaccompanied tour, so the army didn't have a school there. It was well organized, and enough teachers were there to cover the classes. Pete's job was to take care of all finances, running Shalom House, paying the teachers and staff,

129

and all other associated expenses. I'm glad I didn't have that job as the House had several different bank accounts in Korean *wan* and U.S. dollars. The exchange rate varied daily, so it was a constant juggling act. Oh my!

Mr. Ko, the Korean manager of the house and kitchen, was a gem. He ran a short-order food service. The coffee was always hot and, at ten cents a cup, in constant demand.

Shalom House is a three-story brick building that made you feel comfortable as soon as you walked in. There was a big living room with a fireplace, comfortable furniture but nothing fancy (it all looked well used), several card tables, bookcases loaded with all sorts of materials, a TV with a VCR and dozens of tapes, and off to one side, a Ping-Pong table.

No American housewife would tolerate the kitchen, but Mr. Ko loved it, and he and his wife kept it humming.

There was a small guest room and bath on the ground floor, with the rest of the place given to offices and classrooms. The Sansom's apartment was on the second floor along with dormitory/guest room with six beds and a shower for men who were up from Seoul and wanted to spend a night or a weekend. The charge, all of two dollars a night! There were more classrooms and an auditorium on the third floor.

We got home from Korea in time for Thanksgiving with son Jim Bryan, Donna, and Christian in Palm Beach Gardens, Florida; Christmas in Carmel, Indiana, with Pete's daughter, Bonnie and her family—who got the white marble lions; it was out to Montana for an Easter visit with my daughter, Anne, and her family before they left for Hong Kong as missionaries with OMS International.

Sandwiched in with that was scheduling the Witness Season for fourteen Presbyterian churches in February; organizing a family and PYFS Class of '40 reunion in Black Mountain, North Carolina; and sailing for two weeks in the Keys with the Webers. I never thought retirement would be dull but hardly expected so much activity. We figured that as long as the Lord blessed us with good health and opportunities, we were happy to keep going.

We'd sailed with the Webers before and knew we had a good time ahead of us. Mid-June is the season for afternoon thunder storms, and none of them missed us as we sailed south on the Inland Waterway. Our daily encounter with Mother Nature followed a predictable pattern—high winds, rain, flashing lightning, and crashing thunder. It's so violent you never get used to it.

We sailed as far as Key Largo, where Walt left the boat in a private marina. We rented a car and drove the rest of the way to Key West to do the usual tourist things, and it was fun. We met Mel Fisher at his museum that holds all the treasures recovered from various wrecks, took the Conch Train tour of the city, and had some interesting dining experiences. We were fortunate enough to get rooms at the Navy BOQ, costing us four dollars a night. We sure did like those rates.

Back at Key Largo, we went to the Pennykamp Marine Park for the day. Walt took us to a swimming beach so I could try out his scuba gear. That was a blast, but I had a little trouble with my ears when we got down to about fifteen feet. After checking me out, he turned me loose with my promise to stay near by. "Just don't swim off to China, Fran," he warned.

I was in about six feet of water when I picked up a soft yellow object that looked like a sponge about the size of a tennis ball. I noticed some small stones embedded in it. It wasn't anything I wanted to keep so I dropped it. When I returned to the beach the moment my hands were out of the water they began to sting. It felt as if pins were pricking the skin. I should have done something about it right then, but I didn't realize I had a bad sting. By the next day the palms turned bright red and were painful to the touch. Within two days my hands were swollen to about twice their normal size and I could hardly bend my fingers. Needless to say, I was pretty useless in the storms and completely helpless in preparing our meals. What a mess! We had agreed that I'd fix breakfast and lunch, and Dee would do dinner. She got stuck with the whole business. As soon as we went ashore, I checked in with a pharmacist in a drug store. He looked at my hands when I rested them on the counter in front of him.

"I'm sorry, I can't help you," he said as he gently touched my palm. As soon as we got home I went to see Dr. Stewart. He took one look at my hands and put me on a ten-day course of prednisone. Each day there was less pain, but it took three months before they were back to normal. I had tangled with a fire sponge.

On the return voyage we sailed through Snake Cut to the Atlantic Ocean side of the Keys so we could take advantage of the Gulf Stream going north. We headed out into the deep water, whose color is that beautiful dark blue. The Gulf Stream is amazing. It's clearly marked with no fuzzy dividing line; it's knife-edge sharp and a vivid purple. It flows at about two knots, so we made good time. We would have followed it all day, but another thunder storm was moving toward us. Walt thought it the better part of wisdom to go back to the Inland Waterway at Ft. Lauderdale.

Our last night out, we treated the Webers to dinner at the Outrigger in the Frances Langford Marina. We swam in the pool, had hot showers, and dined in the elegant restaurant. It was one of two times that Dee and I wore dresses and the men wore slacks and shirts.

On the 10th of August we flew to Stony Point, New York, for a five-day orientation. Our work in Tong-Du-Chon was sponsored by the Volunteers In Mission (VIM) program of the Presbyterian Church, USA. We were in a group of thirty-five that was going all over the globe, many of them to Egypt for one or two years to teach in a Christian girls' school. Much of the instruction was about the nuts and bolts of living in a foreign land. It was old hat for both of us, but we enjoyed the experience. Pete and I helped with some of the orientation involving countries where we'd lived. Paul Crane, a missionary kid and retired Korea medical missionary, came in for half a day to give us a very good personal-health lecture. We were also impressed with the other staffers from the New York office, particularly Sigmund Rhee, the Far East VIM director. He led the devotions a couple of times, and he was excellent. I could have listened to him all day.

We received word that all systems were go, so we booked a flight on Northwest Airlines, nonstop Chicago to Seoul, on the 28th. Friends who had done it said it was fine. You have two dinners and see two movies and you are there. It left Chicago at 1:40 p.m. and got to Seoul at 5:55 p.m. the next day, but it's just one long thirteen-hour trip. That sounded find to us.

Shalom House

Headquarters, 2nd Infantry Division

Shalom House

It was rather daunting to think of taking over all the programs that the Sansoms were leaving in our hands.

"Just do what you're comfortable with," Julie said, "and leave the rest. We can catch up when we return." That made the job seem manageable, and I gave a sigh of relief.

Friday night we were invited out to our first Korean dinner—a good-bye for Don and Julie and a welcome for us. It was given by a class that I was taking over from Julie, one that I looked forward to three times a week. There were two Korean army doctors, one dentist, a dental assistant, a student, an insurance broker, a Republic of Korea (ROK) army chaplain, a prosecuting attorney, a violinist, and an actor. How about that for a mixed bag?

A couple of weeks later when I started the class I found that their book knowledge was good, but pronunciation was difficult, and they were absolutely lost when it came to idioms. The best text I could find was the *Reader's Digest* because it's written in everyday language and loaded with idioms. Within a couple of weeks they left their shyness at the door and before long were sharing personal stories about their lives and families. It was a rich experience.

The last Sunday afternoon before they left, Don took us on a trip to Soyo San (Soyo Mountain), about fifteen minutes from town. Several GIs and Korean friends went with us. One thing that really impressed us was how clean the streets and parks were. There wasn't a scrap of paper, tin can, bottle, or any other trash on the ground, a real change from what I remembered from former times in Korea. There were hundreds at

Soyo San having picnics, camping, and walking around as we were. The whole area was immaculate.

It took us about half an hour to climb to some pretty temples. The path followed a fast-flowing stream with a number of restaurants at the lower end. One had a most interesting way to keep their customers cool and comfortable on a hot, sunny day. Tables seating eight, complete with umbrellas and chairs were in the stream. Customers sat on the chairs, with their feet in the water. Neat idea. There were a dozen or more tables so arranged farther upstream.

The Koreans, ever curious about foreigners, watched us as we climbed, and I knew they were talking about us when they pointed at me and said, *"hal-muni,"* which means grandmother. I was delighted.

Tables in the stream at Soyo San

One of the first orders of business was to go on base to establish APO privileges and get passes to the PX and commissary. With Pete's military ID and Korean visas showing we would be in country for six months, there was no problem.

The first time we drove up to the 2nd Division gate, a young guard sauntered up to our car.

"Are you folks here as tourists?" he asked, resting his forearm on the door, noting that we were both elderly. Pete handed him his military ID card, and when the kid read his rank, there was an immediate change. He stepped back a pace, stood ramrod straight and saluted.

"Yes sir, Colonel, sir," he said as he raised the gate for us to pass. We laughed all the way to the post office. Soon our car was recognized by those on guard duty, and we never had a problem. They started raising the gate as we approached and saluted smartly as we passed.

Not long after the Sansoms left for the States, one of the teachers asked me to fill in with the kindergarten children because their teacher was sick. The substitute hadn't come yet. I had no idea how I would manage twenty wiggly, squirmy youngsters, but there was nothing to do but try.

Each child perched on a small chair, and at that age they do not sit still for more than two seconds. I began by asking them to tell me their names, how old they were, and how many other children there were in their families. I wondered what to do next; the teacher still wasn't there. Pete's office was just across the hall, so I asked him to come over for a few minutes and give me a hand.

When he came in, the children were still squirming and falling off their chairs until I asked for their attention.

"Okay," I said, "I want you to meet my husband, Col. Peterson." The speed of the reaction was amazing. They sat quietly, with eyes as big as saucers, not a word, not a movement, just awe. We were in a military community, and these were children of enlisted men. It was obvious that they were rank conscious. Even at that young age "Colonel" meant due respect and maybe a little fear.

With hands over their hearts, they repeated the Pledge of Allegiance, and we sang *My Country 'Tis of Thee.* Just as we were singing the last phrase, the substitute arrived. Praise the Lord.

City water is the color of light tea and not safe to drink. One of our jobs was to fill five jerry cans at the base purification plant. Though we needed to do it twice a week at least, it wasn't a problem because we went on base several times a week to pick up our mail.

We didn't have a box; there was a mail bag. Both of us were authorized to collect it.

Shalom House was really jumping from 8:00 a.m. when school started to about 10:00 p.m. when the last English class was over and the last game of Ping-Pong won. Two men covered the kitchen and took care of the house twenty-four hours a day.

Mr. Koo was the day person. He came at 8:00 in the morning and stayed until 9:30 at night when Mr. Lim took over until 8:00 the next morning. On weekends Mr. Lee served. It was a fine arrangement that had things running very smoothly. Mr. Koo had a good command of English, was an elder in the Presbyterian Church just across the street, and the nicest person you'd want to meet. One of our first days he took me to visit two big markets in town so I could see what was available. When I needed good fresh fish or fruits and vegetables, I gave him the money and he'd do the shopping.

The Second Division ("Second to None" their motto) was the most battle-ready division of the whole U.S. Army. The alert was sounded often and always unannounced. Many a time in the midst of a discussion we heard the first notes of the wailing sirens, and off they went. The house was empty of soldiers in less than five minutes. They had to be back with their units in full battle gear in twenty minutes. Did they run!

One day at a time, Pete and I took over the classes that Don and Julie established. Neither of us was a Bible scholar, but we did the best we could. We had such a good experience in Taiwan that we didn't fear what might happen.

Pete's favorite class was a group of Korean pastors and army chaplains. He loved their enthusiasm and the stories they had to tell. He asked how much vacation time they had in a month. One answered, "I don't need time off. Work with young soldiers is so rewarding that I don't take any."

A core group of GIs and Koreans came every Tuesday night. After most of the people had gone home, they wanted an hour of Bible study, singing, and praying. By that time I was really cooked, but they were so enthusiastic we decided to give it a whirl. The Sansoms had a good selection of commentaries that I used to prepare lessons, but I was still tired after a long day. When those young people came in with their guitars and a piano player and we'd sung for twenty minutes or so, I was all hopped up and ready to go. It never ceased to amaze me. All I needed was a little oxygen!

We had a lesson on Matthew 21—Jesus' triumphal entry into Jerusalem.

"How is it," they asked, "that Jesus wanted to ride on a donkey, such a nothing animal? Why not a horse so he would sit up high and everybody could see him?

142

Wouldn't that make him look more important and strong?" Fortunately one of the commentaries helped me with that.

"Riding the donkey was a symbol the Jews would understand," I explained. "A man-of-war rode a horse; the king rode a donkey. In so doing, Jesus was making a statement about himself."

To make the point clear I asked them a question about something with which they were familiar.

"If you saw some cars out there on the street, motorcycles in the lead with their lights on followed by a couple of jeeps carrying armed soldiers, a long black limousine with darkened windows and flags flying up front, with another jeep following it, you'd know for sure that somebody very important was visiting Camp Casey. Isn't that so?" Light dawned!

"Yes," they agreed. "That's the way the big shots travel."

"Jesus knew the people understood the significance of his riding the donkey, that he was declaring himself to be their king."

The biggest scheduled activity of the week was Saturday night. Several men from Camp Casey were in charge of *The Fishermen*, a group of thirty to forty men and women. They chose coming to Shalom House over other activities on base or going to Vill, a street just off base that offered bars, restaurants, and brothels, a universal fixture near military bases.

There was a lesson read followed by lively discussion. We didn't involve ourselves unless asked, and it was interesting to see how they worked through everyday problems. Most of the men were enlisted and often had trouble dealing with difficult officers. They were quick to add that the colonels were pretty good, but those junior officers were a pain in the you-know-what.

The meeting was followed by food, of course, and it was always a big pot of "Christian soup," compliments of Mr. Koo. He started making it the first thing Saturday morning with ham hocks and water. As the day progressed he added everything but the kitchen sink, and it was so good. After smelling it all day, by 9:00 p.m. we were ready for some. Corn chips and cookies were served too, and in my enthusiasm, I offered to bake a cake for anyone celebrating a birthday that week. Guess what? I had to come up with one or two every week.

It wasn't hard to love those young people. For several it was their first time away from home, and Shalom House was a place of comfort for them. As they got used to Pete's being a colonel, they looked on him as a father figure and confided their concerns. Tim (not his real name) was a new Christian who kept calling

Pete about discoveries that excited him while reading his Bible for the first time. Once he was on night watch up at the DMZ, and just had to ask Pete a question at 2:00 in the morning! Oh well. When he got back to town he apologized and promised not to do it again.

Some weeks later Tim came to the meeting in tears, and wanted to talk to Pete in private so they went into his office. He had a wife and baby back in the States and was frantic.

"I've committed the unpardonable sin," he sobbed. "I was just stupid and went to the Vill with some of the guys, and now I've done this terrible thing, and I know God can never forgive me. My wife and baby—I feel so awful. I know it's an unpardonable sin. What can I do?"

Pete just sat with him and listened while he sobbed out his agony, kept him supplied with tissues, and waited.

"Colonel Pete, will you please pray for me?" he asked. "I just don't know how to pray for myself. I don't know how God can hear me."

Pete put his hand on his shoulder and led him in a prayer of repentance, then told him of King David's sin with Bathsheba.

"He not only slept with her, but to cover up the fact that he got her pregnant, he sent her husband into battle and had him stationed where he'd be killed. He added murder to the mix! How about that for big-time sin? Yet after the prophet Nathan confronted him with what he had done, David repented.

"You have your Bible?" Pete asked. Together they read the 51st Psalm in which David asks forgiveness for his sin and God forgives him.

"Even with all that, God called David 'a man after my own heart.' How that's for wiping the slate clean?"

"It's a lot more than I deserve," Tim said. "I hate the idea, but should I tell my wife?"

"Think about it," Pete said. "Let it rest for a time. Why dump it on her? She has enough to handle with a new baby and you over here, doesn't she? Never, never lie to her, so tell her the truth if she asks. Otherwise keep it to yourself. And I'd suggest you get yourself checked out at the clinic. You might have picked up some nasty stuff, and you don't want to take that home to her, okay?"

Tim was feeling very chastened but relieved. Pete felt blessed to be able to minister to the men in their time of need, and always hoped he'd said he right thing.

Fishermen's Meeting

Sunday nights were our responsibility. I carried the load on Tuesday nights, so Pete took it on. It was a smaller group because the chapel program usually had something scheduled.

He often invited one of the chaplains to give his testimony and tell how he decided to serve in the army. It was quite an eye-opener to hear that some of them endured strong family opposition to their entering the ministry, and to be a chaplain was just the end. They served with more than a little personal sacrifice.

After a couple of months, ideas for a good program were in short supply, so Pete suggested we talk about tithing. Having served thirty years in the Air Force and always being involved in a chapel program, he knew what he was talking about. Tithing wasn't a big subject, for all their religious needs were met. There was always a program acceptable to all faiths and a chapel. The collection taken at each service was usually donated to some good cause. As a result the tithe wasn't something they feel an urge to put in their budgets. They just gave as the spirit moved them, usually a dollar or some loose change. The best way to get the message across was to tell his own story. It was Pete's idea, so I said, "Go for it!"

"My experience in planning a budget was much like yours," he began, "housing, food, clothes, entertainment, and so on—maybe even a little for savings, but mostly it got to be a matter of staying ahead of the bills that had a way of piling up fast. After retirement I had a good income and still didn't pay much attention to my bank balance except to make sure I could at least cover the interest on our credit card debt. Do you have any idea how stupid that is? Really dumb.

"When my wife died very suddenly, I moved to Georgia to live with my daughter and her family. Since I didn't have basic expenses I was pretty free with the dollars, but the credit card debt didn't go away. Before Fran and I were married we talked about how we would manage our lives and what we felt was important. The 'second time around' you're a little smarter about these things.

"One day while we were discussing finances she said, 'I believe in tithing. How about you?'

"Oh, I've always been a big spender when it comes to the church," I answered. "Last year I gave $350.

"'Well,' she said, 'that's not exactly what I'm talking about. My understanding is that a tithe is 10 percent of gross pay.' I gulped as I made a quick calculation of what a tenth of mine would be.

"I'll have to think that one over a little," I said. "'I've never done that before, but we can talk about it.'

"'Look, honey,' she answered, 'don't worry. I just want you to know that I tithe anything that comes in to me. Your money's yours; do just what you feel is best.'

"Then Fran went on to quote Malachi 3:10, which says, 'Bring all the tithes into the storehouse, that there may be food in my house. "Test me in this," says the Lord of hosts, "and see if I will not open for you the windows of heaven and pour out so much blessing that you will not have room enough for it." Golly, I hadn't seen that one before. She pointed out that it's the only place in the Bible where the Lord challenges us to put Him to the test! It's something worth thinking about.

"End of discussion, but it wasn't long until I saw the results of how Fran's tithing and money management differed from mine. As a secretary she made a quarter of my pay, but she had her own condo in McLean, Virginia, and a healthy savings account. I wasn't aware of it until we went to Florida to find a place to live. She had money to make the down payment on the condo we chose and another $1,000 to upgrade the carpeting. I didn't.

"After we were married and moved to our new home, it took time for everything to settle down into any sort of routine. At her request I took over the finances. After a month or two I brought up the subject of tithing.

"'How about trying 5 percent to see how it goes,' I asked.

"'Sure, why not,' she said. 'Whatever seems good to you is fine with me.' I gave that amount to Trinity, the church we were attending. After a couple of months I tòld that I never missed the 5 percent, so I'd go for 10. I never missed it either. The trick is to make your tithe the first check of the month, not the last.

"Fran had a small-sized fit when she found out I had quite a large credit card debt. The only way to calm her was to set up a plan to pay it all off, even if we had to eat hamburgers for a couple of months, but we got it done. Oh my, what a relief, and there was peace in the house too." Pete winked at me, and the guys had a good laugh.

"I'm living proof that it really does work. Since then we've been able to pay off the mortgage on our condo and have money to donate to the church and other worthwhile organizations. It's given me a great sense of freedom from money worries."

That was the first time I'd heard Pete spell it out in so many words, and thankfully I saw blessings come equally for both of us.

"There's no way it would work for me," Billy said to Pete after the meeting. "The last two days before pay day I have to borrow money from the Red Cross girls to buy food. How can I give to the church?"

"Okay, you say it can't be done." Pete said. "I say it can. Tell you what. You pay your tithe to your home church, the one you attend in the States. Write a check and send it along with a note. Man alive will they be surprised and happy to hear from you; then pay the rest of your bills. Just keep to your regular spending and at the end of the month if you've run out, let me know and I'll give it to you. It won't be a loan but a gift, okay?"

"That's a deal," Billy said, "but I still don't see how it will work. Money is money, and I know my arithmetic; but gee whiz—it's worth a try." The end of the month came, and you guessed it. He had money left over. We had a new believer. Before he left for the States, Billy had money in the bank for his first semester at Bible School.

As a routine began to develop we decided to follow the Sansoms' plan of taking Wednesdays off and going into Seoul. Driving in Korea is a challenge, and braving the big city after the country life at Shalom House was scary. The first few times we went only to places we knew well, but little by little we ventured to others but not very far off the main road. Because Korea was already getting ready for the Olympic Games, there were many signs in English, a real boon. Whenever we were totally mixed up, we just looked for signs for the airport and got back to familiar ground.

The commissary at Camp Casey was very small, thus all of our big purchases were made in Seoul at Yong San's South Post. It was enormous, one of the largest in the world. Likewise the Chosun Gift Shop run by the Officers' Wives' Club was open two days a week. They carried choice merchandise from all over the Far East. With I'Taewan next door to the base, shopping was indeed a pleasure.

The first couple of times we took film to be developed on base we were together. If ever I went without Pete, the clerk always asked, "Where is grandfather?" They just loved that man.

Occasionally it was more convenient to take the train into Seoul than to drive. We went in the early morning when others were headed into the city to work. If all the seats were taken we stood, holding on to overhead straps. Without fail, within a few minutes I'd feel a tug on my jacket or sleeve, and someone was offering me his seat. Having white hair in Korea has its advantages!

On the whole, GI-related problems were few. Once in a while fights erupted when they had too much to drink, but no more than expected. One night, however, that all changed when two of them murdered a taxi driver.

We felt just sick when we learned what happened. They were out on the town and caught a cab. After telling him to stop in a dark street, they pulled out knives, cut his throat, and as he was bleeding to death they sat there eating his supper. Realizing they might be in big trouble, they decided to leave the taxi and walk back to the main gate. When the guards questioned them about all the blood on their clothes, they said it was from a nosebleed.

The taxi driver was still alive when somebody found him and got him to the hospital. "GI, GI, GI," he said over and over before he died, so they knew where to look for the culprits. The two suspects claimed innocence but soon confessed and were held in the base jail. Because the court-martial process took several days, the Korean community felt not enough was being done to punish the offenders. They staged a demonstration at the main gate. We went to pick up the mail and noticed the crowd, unaware what was going on. Soon thereafter the gate was closed, and nobody could go in or out. The Koreans had the man's body in a bus and wanted to bring it on base in protest, but the MPs weren't about to let that happen. They used tear gas to break up the crowd, and the protesters were given a chance to state their case. After two hours, we were able to leave. The army found the men guilty and turned them over to Korean authorities, who gave them long sentence in a Korean prison.

Dreadful as it all was, it had a better ending. A Baptist missionary ministered to them in prison, helping both of them to become Christians. It didn't change their situation, but it changed them. They apologized to the dead man's family and offered support as they were able to provide it. When it was suggested that perhaps they might get out earlier than expected, they said it no longer mattered. Their lives were full of joy as they witnessed to other prisoners! They were in no hurry to leave.

The 1986 Asian Games held in Seoul put Korea on the map as a major player in world sports. Wrestling was a huge event. The finals were on TV the evening of Pete's pastors' English class and mine for professional people. It was such a big event that we suspended class and watched the contest. All the righteous indignation against the Japanese was embodied in that one man, and how they cheered him on. Every time the Korean was about to pin his opponent, those dignified men were down on their haunches next to the TV, shouting their encouragement and pounding the floor. When it was finally over and Korea won, nothing could contain their jubilation. It was as if once and for all they put the Japanese in their place. The Chinese were on top with the greatest number of gold medals, but the Koreans beat the Japanese, and that was what really counted.

One Sunday afternoon several of us took a trip to Prayer Mountain, a retreat center that functions every day of the year. It's owned and operated by the Full Gospel Church, the largest church in the world, founded by Dr. Cho. As the name indicates, the principal activity is prayer. On the lower level of the largest building, there is a ten-thousand-square-foot room where people come for up to forty days of fasting and prayer. They bring a *yo*, a thin sleeping mat, and a blanket. Men, women, and children are all together. Wherever a person's mat was put down became his space. When we were there it was about half full. With lights turned low, some were sleeping, others were praying out loud or silently. The atmosphere was very worshipful. Those fasting were asked to drink regularly from a well. They called it hallelujah water. A large meeting hall was just above the prayer and fasting room.

Prayer Mountain had an area where there were 150 shelters for private prayer. Each was dug into the side of the mountain, several yards apart, and measured about four by five feet and six feet high. There was a cross sketched on the plastered wall opposite each door, and the one we looked into had a few candle stubs on the floor beneath the cross. It was easy to tell which shelters were occupied because shoes are left outside. Some pray very quietly and others do not. We went past one where there were four pairs of shoes, and all the folks inside were storming heaven with loud prayers. Pete went by one in which a woman was singing. He said her voice sounded like a flute—clear, high, and just beautiful.

There was a building for foreign visitors where rooms could be had for about six dollars a night—four bunks to a room. Some were for women or men with thirty bunks to a room and a cost of three dollars.

As we walked around, several people came up to talk with us. One was a pastor on his way to conduct a service for the "fasters." When we got beyond the introductions, Pete mentioned that I was from North Korea. It turned out that he was from Pyengyang and had come south when he was fifteen. He was happy to meet a fellow northerner. In all conversation there was a lot of "hallelujahing" which is the same in all languages. Like all good things, it is growing and growing. Several new buildings were going up, and it seemed their eighty-nine acres would soon be built up wall to wall.

A pastor in Pete's class asked if we would go out to his country church for Sunday morning services. I was asked to say a few words of greeting before Pete gave his testimony and the pastor translated. I was surprised and delighted at how easy it was to talk for about three minutes without help. I asked how many were from the North, and about half a dozen hands went up. After the service we met the congregation and found that one of the women was also from Syenchun, my home town. Naturally we had our pictures taken.

She was also from Syenchun

The next Sunday we were invited to do the same thing at Mr. Koo's church just across the street from Shalom House. This time it was an evening service, and the place was packed. They have an unusual custom. The family of one of the deacons participates in the service by singing a hymn. That evening a woman and her two children sang *"Jesus Loves Me"*. They just bellowed it out. The little girl, particularly, was giving it her all. She was absolutely precious.

The front rows were filled with the elderly, and I loved watching them. They all looked so small, white haired, glasses perched on the ends of their noses, and as they sang they rocked back and forth. They didn't need to look at their books. They knew all the verses by heart.

November 1 Pete was seventy years old, and we celebrated it with *The Fishermen* Saturday night. I made a big pot of Greek Chicken soup and a cake with seventy-one candles, one to grow on. In Asia the sixtieth birthday is the most important as it completes the golden cycle— five times the twelve years of the zodiac, but seventy comes in a close second. It was wonderful to see how all the young people loved Pete.

We were notified that our visas would have to be extended, something they could not do in Korea. It necessitated a trip out of country. With Taiwan the closest, we flew there on a Sunday and returned the following Friday. We chose to stay at the President Hotel, where we'd lived for three months with IESC, and were warmly greeted by all from the doorman to the hall sweeper. It was like old home week. I guess they remembered Pete's generous tips.

We took advantage of the time to visit granddaughter, Lisa Helsby, at Morrison Academy, half-way down the island in Tai Chung. What a pretty little thing she was, bubbly and enthusiastic. She was thoroughly enjoying boarding school and liked everything except the food; isn't that always the way? It wouldn't be normal not to complain about it.

Both ways we took the two-hour trip in the *gwagwan,* a deluxe, nonsmoking bus, a great relief as there were no smoking restrictions elsewhere. Being in the land of pirated books, I picked up the latest by Wilbur Smith and also James Clavell's *Whirlwind.*

The Sansoms told us before they left that Thanksgiving and Christmas were the hardest times for the troops. Thank heaven we made plans to have as big a celebration as the budget would allow.

Thanksgiving week was devoted to cooking. The local commissary was most helpful in ordering turkeys for me so we didn't have to lug them all the way from Seoul. With a lot of help from Mr. and Mrs. Koo, we prepared turkeys, sweet potatoes, mashed potatoes, vegetables, coleslaw, cranberry jelly, bread and butter, and apple and pumpkin pies.

Mr. Imm was the greatest with the big oriental chopper. He took care of the cabbage for the coleslaw. When I suggested doing it in the food processor, he was having none of it. He'd do it! Mr. Koo did the decorating and arranged the tables—and took care of anything else that came along.

The turkeys were cooked Wednesday and put in baggies in amounts to heat up in a few minutes in the microwave. The stuffing was abundant and the gravy plentiful as was everything on the menu, but we ran out of dressing and gravy way too soon. For Christmas dinner we did better, but again we had to scrape the pan for the last couple of helpings of gravy! The whole house was decorated; a roaring fire in the fireplace attracted chilly guests, and the mood was festive. As people arrived they went past the serving window and received a generous helping of everything. Pete and I seated them, made sure they had what they wanted to drink, and kept things moving. As soon as one table finished, we set it up for the next in line. Thankfully we had enough for all. At Thanksgiving we counted 84. Evidently word got around that Shalom House was the best place—we had 115 for Christmas. There were several dining halls on base that served holiday meals, all free, but we were gaining a great reputation for hospitality.

Several of the men wanted to put on a harvest party for the Indian Head School children and asked if I'd do some of the cooking (it turned out to be all the cooking). Between the two of us, Mr. Koo and I made three cakes, a laundry basketful of popcorn balls, and fifteen pumpkin pies. He's the fastest man I have ever seen with a rolling pin. He'd have the crust rolled out so quickly I could just about get the edge crimped on one before he'd have the next ready. Let me tell you, with help like that life was pretty easy.

On Sunday mornings, Pete and I sang with the choir at Stone Chapel during the 11:00 a.m. service. Once a month children from an orphanage did the honors. An officer and his wife who also attended said they wanted to do something special for the youngsters at Christmas and had put money aside for them each time they sang.

"We hesitate to give it to the woman in charge," they said, "for fear it will end up in the general pot. We'd be thankful if you'd take care of distributing some small gift to each child."

"We've had quite a bit to do with the orphanage and will be glad to help," I said. They gave $140, a generous amount, and we added another $60 to make an even $200. Mr. Koo called to find out how many children there were, their ages, and sex. We got bags and a variety of small candy bars at the PX. Mr. Koo got tangerines and *yut*, a Korean taffy, at the market, and we added a banana for each. We took the remaining money and put it in envelopes for the forty-nine children, each with names on them. Those under five got W1,000; ages six to ten, W2,000; and the forty-one over ten got

161

W3,000 apiece. At W865 to U.S.$1 it wasn't a lot, but when one little kid opened the envelope and saw the cash, he exclaimed, "Ton!" (money), we knew we'd made a hit. Pete and I had the joy of delivering it all at 11:00 a.m. on the 24th of December.

On Christmas Eve we went to a service at the Stone Chapel, after which we went caroling around the base. About a half hour was all we could tolerate in the intense cold. We ended up at one of the recreation centers for hot cocoa and cookies. The evening was still young, so a bunch of us, two with guitars, went to the Vill to sing. It was an experience I'll not soon forget. We stood next to a wall at the junction of three streets where we wouldn't hinder traffic or block business entrances. The condition of many of the men was rather sad. Hearing the singing, they came around to listen, and some joined in. One who was already three sheets to the wind said to his buddies, "Now come on, guys, it's time to get serious about Christmas." They stopped for quite a long time, sang with us, and before they wandered off, two of them came over to give me a hug. It was nice to be a mother figure in times like that.

During our stay at Shalom House, the group went to the Vill to sing several times. I was always amused when we sang one of their favorite choruses that starts with, "*Come to the water; stand by my side. I know you are thirsty and won't be denied. "* The major activity there being drinking, it hit a funny bone.

We went back to Shalom House for an 11:00 p.m. Communion service conducted by one of our chaplains. It was a beautiful time with the lights on the tree, friends gathered to worship, all joined together by the common bond of loneliness in being away from family but celebrating with the larger family of God.

Tony's story has probably been duplicated thousands of times the world over when our men in uniform find themselves in foreign lands and there are poor, unattended children around.

Tony ran with a gang of street boys. He was a really nice-looking youngster, and several men from Shalom House took an interest in him. They kept him clothed, gave him a little cash and a lot of love. His mother ran away when he was a baby, and his father was in an institution. A half brother would have nothing to do with him. He'd been in several orphanages but always ran away.

These kids knew how to beg, steal a little, get food from restaurants, and talk GIs into renting rooms for them on really cold nights. They all slept together. Mike and Sunny Brady, one of our young couples, took him home several times to make sure he didn't spend the night on the street. They also looked into placing him in an orphanage and lined up a job for him. He was only fourteen, but he needed to be anywhere but on the street if he wasn't to end up in jail. One Sunday night several of the Korean women sat Tony down for a serious talk. They told him he had to choose what he wanted to do because he couldn't continue to live as he was. It turned out he didn't want the orphanage or a job. He wanted to keep on being helped by the GIs and taken in by Shalom House people from time to time, but he wanted to have his life on the streets, too. Well, that was that. Mike went to their apartment and got a grocery bag of Tony's things and gave it to him and told him good-bye. He was one startled kid. He begged to stay at their place that very cold night, but they said no. The poor kid cried all the way down the lane to the street, and Sunny and Mike were just as badly broken up over it. But they and we felt there was no other choice.

When they got back to their apartment, Tony was there and said he had changed his mind and did want the job in Seoul. Mike told him, fine, that if he hadn't changed his mind in the morning to come on back. They didn't take him in as he'd hoped. I guess that one last night on the street did it. He went to them at eleven the next morning and said yes to the job. They went right away, and took him to the dingy, cramped little factory. After introducing him to the family who owned it, a good, friendly bunch, they left him. As they departed he was fighting back tears, but we hoped it would be a new beginning for him. Tony was young enough and smart enough to change. The others in the gang were so tough they wanted nothing except your money, any way they could get it.

With Christmas past, the New Year was not far off. On New Year's Eve the usual group came for an evening of fun and games followed by a Watch Night service. Our favorite chaplain from the base conducted a Communion service that ended right at twelve o'clock. What a good way to start the New Year!

Some of the group from Pennsylvania insisted that the first food consumed in the New Year had to be sauerkraut and hot dogs. I'd ever heard of it, but they insisted. As soon as the last song was sung and the last "amen" spoken, the feast was on. Everybody seemed to enjoy it, but I'm not from Pennsylvania, and I'm glad. You can have my share.

At my first English class for professionals after the New Year, we talked about important things that had taken place in 1986. I then asked each one to tell what he looked forward to in 1987. Three of the ten present said they wanted to know Jesus Christ, and an artist, who was already a Christian, said she wanted to begin study to be a missionary. Let me tell you, that really made my day. All of those young people became very dear to me; it was hard to leave them.

You can never anticipate all the things you'll be asked to do in a job like that. A first for Shalom House was a wedding. You could almost call it an "instant wedding." An Soon, one of the Korean girls, and Harry Salt, a Native American, had been going together for some time. Wedding plans had been on and off again for several months, when one evening An Soon came to see us. She and Harry had been married at City Hall but wanted a Christian ceremony and wondered if they could have it here. Would we ask one of the chaplains to tie the knot? They also wanted it to happen in only six days. I figured we could take care of things on this end. Harry had the duty Sunday, but An Soon met us at the Stone Chapel, and Pete introduced her to Chaplain Heath. He arranged to talk with them Monday morning, and decided he could marry them. The happy couple came to talk with me.

"We want an American wedding and reception," they said.

"Okay, we can do that," I agreed. "We can prepare the hall on the third floor and have light refreshments, a wedding cake, punch, nuts and mints, and perhaps a tray of sandwiches. How does that sound to you?"

"That's fine," they agreed. "Just a few people coming so that's okay. You think you can do this for us?"

"I'll be glad to. It will require some extra work for Mr. Koo, so may I suggest you give him a gift?"

"Sure, sure," Harry agreed, "and we'll bring the cake, too. I can order it at the bakery on base. Thank you so much. We really appreciate your help on such short notice. There will be a big feast at Soon's parents' house in the evening; light refreshments will be good."

Friday night we had a rehearsal, walked through the service twice, and all went like clockwork. The wedding was scheduled for 2:00 p.m. the next day.

Mr. Koo and I set up several tables At 1:00, the cake was delivered. Mr. Koo had mixed the punch and set it up with cups and napkins at one end of the table when several of An Soon's brothers arrived with a mountain of food—sliced cold pork, three varieties of rice cakes, and *chop chai,* a kind of fried noodles with meat and vegetables. They plunked huge restaurant-type stainless steel trays on the table, but there wasn't enough room to accommodate all of them. Even when we took the punch off and put it on another table, there wasn't enough space. I rushed downstairs, and between some of the Sansoms' platters and others from the Shalom House supply, we were able to get what we needed for the added food. They looked at me with blank, unbelieving stares when I told them to please arrange the food on the plates. They laughed when I said that their cardboard boxes and steel trays had no *moyong* (good appearance). It was a bit crowded, but not half bad when finished. They were pleased, too.

Everybody but the bride arrived ahead of time. The guests packed the hall, but still no An Soon. We weren't worried—being on time wasn't exactly a Korean virtue. Finally at about 2:30 she arrived in a beautiful satin-and-lace gown, all fixed up in modern Korean style. They really do go all out on the hair and makeup, and each bride looks like every other Korean bride. Their faces are heavily made up, but the hair is something else. It is curled and sprayed in place, and nothing on earth could make it come down. Curly wisps are plastered on her cheeks, and a short, curly fringe goes all around her face, behind which is pinned the flower piece that holds the veil. The headpiece is done in white artificial flowers with all sorts of white-and-silver stems that protrude above the flowers, making a little forest of stems sticking up. I know that sounds terrible, but the effect is really quite pretty.

We sang one hymn. I had Miss Mok, the school secretary, type out the words in English, and she wrote them in Korean, too, so everybody could sing.

The service went off beautifully. Another custom which the Koreans insist on is that the bride, groom, father of the bride, and the minister wear white gloves. It wasn't a problem until they came to the exchange of rings. Chaplain Heath fumbled a little but didn't drop them. They didn't know what to do with the bride's flowers, so they passed them back and forth while each of them struggled to get the gloves off and on again.

There was a lot of food left over, and I had high hopes that we could take it to the orphanage, but no such luck. Before the guests had all departed the brothers dumped what remained into the stainless steel trays and left. They had a big crowd to feed at home!

Now that I have learned a few things, it's too bad I won't have another wedding to arrange.

An Soon, the Bride

One thing that nearly undid us was the last Saturday night at the Fishermen's Fellowship. We sang for an hour before someone gave a devotional message. This time they gave us a "love roast." They presented us with a beautifully embroidered and framed Fisherman's logo, and each told us how much he loved and appreciated us! It was something when Mark, a big strapping sergeant, could hardly talk for being all choked up. His chin quivering, he wiped the tears from his eyes and complained that he was having trouble with his sinuses. They are a precious group, and we can appreciate better what pastors must feel as they move from one church to another. Wonderful, but tough.

The Sansoms returned from the States on January 17, well rested and much pleased with what we had done in their absence. When the books were balanced, Pete showed an overage of twenty-five cents! On our part we were enriched by our experiences at Shalom House and thankful for the opportunity to serve.

Our job done, on the twentieth we packed up and flew back to the U.S. The trip was long, but it was good to be back with family and friends in our own home and in our own bed!

After gaining a little distance from the time in Shalom House, we can say that it was all good. Pete did a fantastic job with the finances and management. I'm so proud of *my man.*

What's next? We weren't sure, but one thing we did know was that we were hooked and looked forward to more volunteer missionary assignments whenever and wherever and the Lord sent us.

Home Again 1987 - 1988

In the first week of March, Pete, Anne Campbell, and I went to the flea market in Deland early one morning. We walked around and shopped for only an hour and a half when Pete complained of being awfully tired. On the way home we stopped at a park to eat a picnic lunch. Though pleasant, it was windy and Pete began to feel cold. As soon as we got home he went straight to bed. During the evening, he had a hard chill followed by a fever, though it wasn't very high. In twenty-four hours it was all over. We thought he probably had some sort of flu. The next day he had swelling in his lower right leg and a red rash on the calf. By the next morning, Saturday, the swelling was severe, and the rash had spread to the front of the leg. That isn't a good day to go the emergency room. Waiting is forever, but finally a doctor saw him and announced that he had phlebitis and needed to be hospitalized immediately. I wanted to take him to Patrick in our car, but they were having none of it and took him in an ambulance. Heparin was started right away, but things didn't go well. He complained of pain in his right hip and was treated for gas. When he was in great pain in the middle of the night they transported him to Cape Canaveral Hospital for tests that showed hemorrhaging into his abdomen! I was at Patrick the next morning when they brought him back, and I was shocked at his appearance. He was deathly white with a greenish tinge. They gave him four units of blood and for four days they kept the IVs going. He had nothing to eat but wasn't hungry. Every couple of days they sent him back to the hospital until the scan showed the hemorrhaged blood was all absorbed. The whole thing wasn't fun. Pete recovered quickly and in no time we planned to drive to Carmel, Indiana, for Easter with Bonnie, Luke, and the children.

The year was filled with visiting the family, work at Trinity as an ordained elder and chairman of the Global Missions committee, attending mission conferences in other presbyteries, and going on several lay witness missions (LWM) under the leadership of Walt Weber.

On the way to one such mission, I stopped at the optometrist to be fitted with my first contact lens. I had just one in my left eye for reading. Distance with my right eye was perfect, but adjusting to the different functions of each eye took a little time.

Our first meeting at the host church was on Friday afternoon. Visiting witnesses and members of the church had a get-acquainted meeting at which we sat around tables, exchanged names, and looked at the program for the weekend. As I studied the schedule, I closed my right eye so I could focus better with the left. When I looked up the man across the table winked at me! He must have thought I was flirting with him.

In October we had a Lampe family reunion at the Red Rocker Inn in Black Mountain, North Carolina. Since our last reunion, we had served at Shalom House, and Molly and Harwood had returned from their stint in Taigu, Korea. He taught radiology in the Presbyterian Hospital, and Molly had several English classes for medical students.

When learning a foreign language it's easy to make mistakes with words that are correct but differ in common usage. One of Harwood's students had a class with Molly as well.

"My English has improved a lot," he said to Harwood, "since I became intimate with your wife." Oh my. We have to wonder how many blunders we made when speaking Korean.

During the year we had extra special times with two of our grandchildren. Jim and Donna went on a three-week trip to Singapore to check out a job opportunity, and we kept Christian. What a lively little one he was—just like his dad. Katie Cronyn, my son Edwin's daughter, came for a visit from Baltimore. At fourteen she was a beautiful young woman, and it was our first chance to have time alone with her. It was such a gift and made me sad that we live so far apart.

In June we took a trip north to see the Staley family. Bonnie underwent surgery the month before and came through with flying colors, but you know fathers. Pete wanted to check on his daughter to make sure she was as well as they said.

While there, we visited the OMS headquarters at Greenwood, Indiana, on the south side of Indianapolis. Carmel isn't far away. For some time Pete and I had our application in with OMS to volunteer in Hong Kong as mission host and hostess. Many people who contribute to OMS travel to Hong Kong and want to see the missionaries they are supporting. One weekend Anne made five trips to the airport meeting people or seeing them off. A regular diet of that sort of schedule can drastically cut into time for language study and missionary work; we thought we might be of some help.

Upon our return home, we received a letter from OMS saying that the day after we visited them an urgent request came from OMS director in Seoul asking if we could go there to do that very thing. A trip to the Orient often included a stopover in Korea, where the small OMS staff was beginning to feel the pinch as more and more people included them in their itinerary. We filled out the forms, sent them in, and planned to discuss the matter with J.B. Crouse, the Korea field director, during the international conference July 6-11. It went well. With our Shalom House experience such a positive one, we felt a strong pull to go back to Korea.

In August we received the invitation to join them in Seoul as honorary missionaries. Immediately the wheels began to turn to meet the October 3 departure date.

I got missionaries lined up for Trinity's next Witness Season and turned the job over to another on the committee. We helped Heydon and Mary celebrate their fiftieth wedding anniversary and saw another chapter in Jim, Donna, and Christian's lives close. A new one opened when they moved from Florida back to Greenville, South Carolina, for a job with DEC.

The first order of business was getting our bodies into shape, eyes examined, and teeth checked. Troubling Pete was a very high platelet count. Evidently 400,000 to 500,000 is normal, but when his went to over 1,000,000 he was sent to a hematologist. The good news was that the count went down again, and there were no bad signs in the bone marrow. That test scared me half to death.

When we were in Thailand in 1981, Pete went with a group up the jungle mountain on the Cambodian side of the Thai border to visit Sok San. On the very steep, narrow path he tripped on a vine and trying to break his fall, he put out both hands. His left hand went down hard on a thorn bush. After they reached the top of the mountain, a Cambodian medic pulled out a dozen or so thorns, but missed one. Pete felt it every so often. Because it wasn't bad enough to do anything about, he left it alone. Several years later a lump appeared on the back of his hand. Still no problem, but in time it grew to the size of a large pea, and it hurt when he bumped it. It seemed like a good idea to have it looked at. Before Pete went into the office surgery, I told him I wanted to see what was inside the lump. The doctor cut open the tumor and found two thorns that he presented to me on a piece of gauze! It reminded me of when we were living in Peking when Edwin was five. When his tonsils were removed, they gave them to me on a piece of gauze. Got to keep all your body parts!

Tickets in hand, we made one last tour around to check on the family. Ending up in Chicago, we spent the night in a hotel near the airport. The next day we were off to Seoul.

OMS Seoul, Korea 1988 - 1993

At the OMS gate

From the fall of 1988, when the Olympic Games were ending, to late 1993, we served as honorary missionaries (doesn't that sound nice?) with the Oriental Missionary Society in Seoul. The mission has retained that name, but its ministry now reaches forty-three countries all around the globe.

We were assigned a house formerly occupied by Elmer and Ella Ruth Kilbourne. Spaced around the compound were six identical houses built after the Korean War from an award-winning design. The layout was beautiful. The living room and adjoining dining room were generous in size as was the kitchen with its many cupboards. The three bedrooms and two baths were well arranged, and there was a lot of closet space. What more can you want? Additionally it boasted a full basement with recreation room and bath, garage, and storage room. Our house was built on a steep hill, so the lower level had doors and windows opening on a patio.

J. B. Crouse, Korea field director, and his wife, Bette, lived about a hundred yards away. The two houses were connected by a footpath that saw a lot of use. Two other houses on our level and another lower down the hill were rented out. The Sandozes occupied the one just below us. They were the only family at the time who had small children—two sons and an adopted Korean daughter. At that same level was a six-unit apartment building.

The singles lived in four of the apartments. Flo Epp was JB's secretary, Trudy Higbee and Susan Truitt were English professors at the Seoul Theological University, and Carol Mitchell was professor of church music and choir director. Later Mark and Jayme Capin and their four lively young ones moved into a house on the other side of the apartments. Mark taught seventh grade at Seoul Foreign School, an American-run school, though a good portion of the students were Koreans who had lived abroad and held foreign passports. Korean nationals are required by law to attend Korean schools.

Truly it was a lovely place to live, and we looked forward to what lay ahead. Every Thursday evening we had a mission prayer meeting. There was a devotional followed by a time of discussion on any and all subjects that concerned us, followed by prayer. Pete and I were Presbyterians, the Sandozes Quakers, and all the rest Methodists. Some kidding developed about the mix as time went on. In JB's enthusiasm over the Korean Evangelical Holiness Church, with which OMS was associated, he went on and on about their tremendous work. All true, but I had to remind him from time to time that the Presbyterians were still the largest and strongest church in the country. Soon JB began to say during announcements, "Fran will be glad to know that . . ." and then told of some praiseworthy thing the Presbyterians were doing. It got to be a joke we all enjoyed.

There was a nice big fireplace in our family room. The "girls," as we called them, usually went out on the town Friday nights. There were good restaurants and often great concerts, plays, or movies to enjoy. On cold winter nights, though, it was much nicer to stay home. Frequently Flo called to propose our making a big fire and some popcorn; she would bring a video. They were available for rent in many shops, and I knew how she hated anything that wasn't all sweetness and light.

"Sure, come along, but be sure to get a movie with plenty of sex and violence," I teased.

J.B. and Bette Crouse

The OMS team

Opportunities for service were many, but our chief job was to take care of visitors from abroad who came to see the missionaries they supported, the seminary, and as much of the country as possible. The compound was a twenty-minute drive from the airport (ten minutes for JB) with light traffic compared to that of the city. There were two guest units in the apartment building. Our assignment was to get them ready for visitors and clean them up afterwards to be ready for the next arrivals.

We were much amused when our granddaughter, Seana, was visiting from the States. We put one batch of guests on the plane in the early afternoon with another due that evening.

"I could use some help in changing the beds and cleaning the bathrooms," I said to Pete.

"You give maid service?" Seana asked in disbelief. "You really do give maid service?"

"Sure, why not?" I asked. "If you'd like to help, some fresh-cut flowers would be nice to have in the living rooms. There are vases down there and a lot of flowers in the compound. Want to come?" Once she got over the shock of what her grandparents were doing, she pitched in, making the job that much easier.

After a time it got to be second nature. We could do it with one hand tied behind our backs—change the beds; fresh linens in the bathrooms after tubs, basins, and toilets were cleaned; new bath soap; a blast of air freshener. Restocking the refrigerator; washing dishes and pots and pans if needed, empty the garbage and wastepaper baskets; more air freshener; a quick once-over-lightly with the dust cloth, a thorough vacuuming; another blast with the air freshener, and we were done. Two or three pairs of hands could accomplish it all in half an hour. It always felt so good to gather up the linens to be washed, close the door, and know that the next weary travelers had a clean, pleasant place to rest.

If there were too many people to accommodate in the apartments, one of the resident families housed them.

Two of the most popular activities were a trip to the Demilitarized Zone, the border between North and South Korea, and visiting I'Taewan, a three-block shopping street and bargain-hunter's paradise. Many high-end shoes and handbags made in Korea could be purchased at a fraction of the U.S. cost. Reeboks sold for eight to ten dollars; one could buy Precious Moments figurines for two dollars; beautiful sweaters were available for eight to ten dollars; suits and shirts were made to order at bargain-basement prices. We bought Dooney-and-Bourke handbags for fifteen dollars and beautiful Gund stuffed animals for five to ten dollars. Native Korean merchandise was highly valued too—eelskin purses, briefcases, wallets, and even shoes. Truly, it was a shopper's dream.

With the men not too interested in shopping, Pete took them to Dunkin' Donuts for coffee while I took the women to find the things on their lists. It usually included a trip to the shoe store.

Stores at I'Taewan were not elegant shops. They were what we'd call holes-in-the-wall. My favorite shoe store was not more than five hundred square feet, storage space and all; but it had everything, and the staff was most helpful. One morning when I had a whole bunch to look after, I spoke to the clerk in Korean to help him understand their requests. His English was not the greatest.

"Why don't you quit talking to us in that North Korean slang," the shop owner said. I was startled when he spoke to me that way with a deep scowl on his face. He looked really angry.

"I'm so sorry," I apologized in Korean. "I didn't mean to offend you, but I'm from North Korea. I was born in Syenchun. My parents were missionaries."

"Oh, is that so," he answered, softening. "Do you want to go back there?" he demanded, a little of the anger showing again.

"Certainly. I'd love to see my birthplace once more, but I wouldn't want to live there."

"Do you like South Korea?" he asked a little more softly.

"Oh yes, we like Seoul very much and are most happy to be here."

"Au, au," he said, stroking my forearm. "Thank you, thank you."

It was so silly that we started giggling. He was talking to me in English and I was answering in Korean with a northern accent. After that, every time I entered his shop or even walked by the windows, he waved and called out, *Peyengyang hal-muni* (North Korean grandmother).

Pete and I had commissary and base exchange privileges, which came in handy and saved us a lot of money. Imported items were still expensive in the market, and military prices were low. They had excellent services too, and I was delighted when I found that they had factory-authorized service for Macintosh computers. I was the proud owner of the latest model, a Mac Plus. I mean it was really the best. When I began to have problems with it, I turned it over to the service department just before we began a two-week English for Ministry and Missions seminar. During that time we lived, ate, and played with the students in English. There were about forty seminary students and pastors who came, wanting to improve their language skills.

At the end of the first week I checked the BX to see if the computer was ready, but it hadn't come back from the workshop in Inchon. I checked again at the end of the seminar. Still no Mac. After being put off several times, I demanded that they bring it back, and eventually it came with a cracked case! It looked as if it had been dropped on a corner that now had little cracks radiating from it. I asked to see the manager, and pushing a cart with the computer in it, was shown to his office.

"I want to see the paper work on this," he announced. Standing there were a couple of clerks and the man in charge of the repair shop. They were all examining the ceiling.

"Do we have a new Mac Plus on the floor," he asked?"

"Yes, sir, we do" came the reply.

"Give it to the lady," he ordered. Hot dog, I got a new computer!

The OMS compound was on the side of a fifteen-hundred-foot hill. It reached to within a hundred yards of the summit and was enclosed with a barbed-wire fence.

The other three-quarters of the hill were public property developed as a park. Along paths to the top were various exercise stations where bars and posts are located to encourage climbers to challenge their muscles and stretch out the kinks. At the very top was a quarter-acre area leveled off and paved with flagstones. A structure in the center honoring some public figure looked like a miniature Washington monument. Walking to the top of the hill was a daily goal that got me ready for the day. Rain or shine, I allowed time to climb it. I returned to the compound feeling as if I could whip my weight in wildcats.

It's a Korean custom not to look strangers in the eye as you pass. Instead, you drop your eyes. Since I'm elderly and have white hair, I chose to break the rule, and spoke to everybody, greeting each one with, "Good morning." At first they gave me a half-smile and looked away, but before long they looked up and answered in English or Korean. It was wonderful. I saw a lot of smiling faces every morning. Several greeted me with "Hallelujah" to let me know they were Christians.

One morning as I reached the top, I found three elderly women sitting on the curb. Just for fun I decided to teach them the "high five." They were not the sort who were likely to know any English, so speaking in Korean I remarked, "You've done very well to come this far. It's a steep hill and not easy to climb." Then I asked if they ever watched sports on TV. They nodded and smiled, so I continued. "When the athletes do very well, don't they do this?" I demonstrated. Yes, they agreed. I explained what it meant. Taking one of them by the wrist, I did the high five with her then with each of the others. They thought it hilarious, and started doing it together, laughing all the while.

"Every time you come up here you can give one another high fives in congratulations," I said.

Well, it began to catch on with many of the daily climbers to the point where my right hand was well exercised and quite red. On one of my last mornings in Korea, Flo went along with me and decided to count the times I gave or received "five." How about seventy-six! The nice thing was that many of the Koreans initiated the greeting.

During our years in Seoul we made several trips back to the States for medical reasons, and each time we returned I was greeted like a long-lost cousin when I began climbing the hill again.

After years of unresolved problems, Bonnie and Luke were divorced on March 29, 1990.

Seoul Theological University had English classes at all levels and tapes to go along with the lessons. They are particularly helpful for beginners and were much in demand, but they didn't last very long. Pete's basso voice was easy for students to understand, and he was pressed into making quite a few. They were kept as masters from which they could make copies as needed.

One day Susan Truitt told us how amusing it was to hear students imitate Pete's pronunciation and his low-pitch tone.

Pete makes language tapes

The subject of U.S. continued involvement in Korea kept popping up. Not a few Koreans wished we'd be gone but were helpless to do anything about it except protest and demonstrate from time to time.

About once a year Trudy Higbee and Susan Truitt asked us to come to their English conversation classes and let the students ask us questions. We were always happy to do so. They particularly liked to talk to Pete. He had a comfortable grandfatherly look, and although they knew he was a retired colonel, they didn't feel intimidated. They just loved him. They liked me too because I was born in Korea.

We were asked the usual things about how old we were, where did we live, how many children did we have and so forth. Without fail someone asked, "Why don't you get your troops out of Korea? We don't want them here any more!"

"We, too, look forward to the day they can come home," Pete answered. "It's a matter to be handled by our governments, and the sooner we can leave the better. I pay pretty high taxes to maintain bases in Korea. I'm sure they would go down if we could pull out of foreign countries." That pretty much took the wind out of their sails.

"What do your parents and grandparents think about the presence of U.S. troops?" I asked. "Do they want them to stay or go?"

"Oh no, oh no!" came the quick answer. "They want them to stay. They lived through the Korean War and they know how bad it was."

It was always thus. Not a family was untouched when hundreds of thousands died and the cities were laid waste during the war. But the young have no such memory and feel their freedom is being denied. In time they'll learn.

My work at the seminary was helping Dr. John Cho, its president, with his English language correspondence and transcribing his taped lectures. It was a thorough education in Wesleyan theology, but I had to challenge him on some of his statements. In one of his lectures he said that his mother-in-law was a wonderful Christian woman, but she was brought up in the Presbyterian tradition. Later when we were having lunch together I asked him what he meant by the big, loud BUT. We had a good laugh.

J.B. and Dr. John Cho

During one of our last years with OMS we attended an All-Asian convocation held in a Presbyterian church in Seoul. Delegates came from all over the Middle and Far East as well as observers from many Western countries to work out ways to cooperate in spreading the Gospel. For many years, the hard work was done by missionaries from the West. Now that the church was well established, it was time for them to take a major part in evangelizing their corner of the world.

The opening ceremonies included a parade of flags representing each country present. Near the end of the line came one lone delegate carrying the Kuwaiti flag. When he entered the hall, the whole body rose to their feet and clapped him all the way to the front. It was a stirring sight!

Each morning began with a worship service and presented a speaker from a different country. The master of ceremonies was a Korean. All addresses were in English or had a translator. The Japanese had the largest delegation. The morning it was their turn to lead, their members sat in a block right in the middle of the hall. The speaker said his message was one of sorrow and asked forgiveness of all the countries his had harmed. In 1910 Japan occupied Korea. In 1937 they invaded the coastal cities of China and wreaked havoc on most. Following Pearl Harbor they swept like a typhoon through the Pacific Rim countries all the way to Australia before they were stopped and turned back by the U. S. military forces. Everyone present was well aware of all that, and anger still burned hot in many a breast.

"We apologize for our country. We are so sorry. Please forgive us. We are so sorry." As the gentleman made these final remarks the Japanese stood together, heads bowed, silent. It was the most stirring moment of the whole conference.

The next day as the service opened, the Korean MC began with, "Yesterday the Japanese were our fellow Christians. Today they are our brothers." The applause was thundering!

Always ready and eager to give credit to the Koreans, JB was showing a guest from the States around the massive building. All delegates stayed in nearby hotels but had their meals at the church. To accommodate them, one floor of the attached garage was made into a dining hall. The floor was painted green, tarps were hung to keep out dust and heat, and a massive air conditioner cooled delegates and workers. All meals were buffet style, with tables set and ready for a hundred at a time. The service was fast, the food excellent, and anyone who wanted to could eat and be out of there in a half hour.

"These Koreans really know how to do things with class," JB remarked.

"Well, would you expect anything less?" I asked. "After all this is a Presbyterian church."

"Oh, Fran," he exploded. "Yes, they are Presbyterians, and yes, they are really good, but so are all Korean Christians.

Over several years Pete's eyes deteriorated to the point where he could no longer drive, and it became my job. For some time we hoped that laser treatment could fix his macular degeneration, but that was not to be. Giving up driving was probably one of the toughest things he ever did. For a man it must be much harder than it is for a woman, because when he gives up driving he looses a lot of his independence. Once he got used to the idea it wasn't too bad; I was always available to my sweet man. I thought of myself as a good driver, but it didn't take long to have my shortcomings pointed out.

One morning while we were on a trip in the States, we had no more than gotten under way when he had a whole lot of criticism about my driving skills in heavy beltway traffic. The poor guy couldn't help me with signs, so I wasn't going very fast lest I miss a turnoff. When it was time to have a little peace in the car, I pulled off the road and announced that if he didn't like my driving, he could walk!

I guess he didn't realize what a pest he was being and that in his frustration was taking it out on me. Right away he apologized, which made us both feel better. After a few slow and easy "smooches" we got under way again.

How do you describe Seoul traffic? It was crowded and dangerous, and we never left the compound without praying first. Where four lanes were marked on the pavement, there were usually five or six lanes of traffic if the shoulders were wide enough. And it was fast.

One of our regular routes into Seoul involved merging with a major highway and doing it without being crushed. I found a way to overcome the problem that worked every time. I drove as close to the heavy traffic as was safe, rolled down the window, and sticking my head out made eye contact with the other driver, asking if he'd let me in. The elderly are given respect in Korea, and if you have white hair it's that much better. It was wonderful. The other driver waved me in, and away we went! As bad and dangerous as it was, nobody ever touched my fender, though there were close calls.

One morning on our way to the All Asia Convocation, our car just died. We were on the downward slope of a very busy bridge, and I was in the middle of three lanes. Cars were whizzing past me so fast that I couldn't pull over into the right lane and get off the road at the bottom of the bridge. A bus driver behind me saw my predicament, pulled into the right lane and stopped, effectively blocking the traffic so I could move. Bless his heart! Love that man. When I was a child in Korea, an unwritten law was that you never passed a car in trouble without stopping to help. Of course in those days there were just bull-cart tracks and absolutely no pavement except for a few streets in

Seoul and Pyengyang. All help was welcomed. It seemed some of that courtesy was remembered.

Since coming to Korea, Pete acquired some new titles. When we were at Shalom House, Mike Brady, one of our regulars, was taking a correspondence course from a Bible School. They asked him for the name of a responsible person who could receive and administer the final exam. Mike gave them Pete's name and address. The exam papers were mailed to Rev. Col. Peterson. At OMS he was known as Col. St. Pete.

One week we were asked to attend a service Saturday morning at the little chapel in the King Sejung Hotel, where a young woman was to receive her Ph.D. The man making the request was one of our EMM students in 1990 and was now a Presbyterian minister. Nothing urgent was going on, so we went.

We arrived at the appointed hour, only to find that Pete was to make the presentation. The degree was from the International Theological Seminary in Van Nuys, California, and since she couldn't be there at graduation, Pete was to act on behalf of John Stranger, Ph.D., president. Pete couldn't read the certificate without his glasses and magnifying glass. I read it for him after which he gave a short talk and made the presentation. It all went well, but the funny part was that they insisted Pete wear the proper garments: a robe, Ph.D. hood, and cap. It got our funny bones so much that it took all we had to keep from laughing out loud. But I have pictures to prove to you that Pete is indeed Col. C. R. Peterson, Ph.D. It could only happen here! I helped the young lady put on the robe before Pete put the hood and cap on her. Everybody was delighted.

In mid-April we had an eleven-day trip to Beijing, meeting up with my sister Molly and her husband, Dr. Harwood Sturtevant, who were living in Xian, China. When things became normalized between the two countries, a plane trip between Seoul and Beijing takes forty-five minutes to an hour. This trip took sixty hours, but it was a good one.

First came the overnight ferry from Inchon to Weihai. We had to sleep on the matted floor, and the john was way down the hall. It was unisex and not very nice. We were not well rested the next day. After exploring their parks and bazaars, we took an hour-and a-half taxi ride to Yontai, had a nice dinner in the hotel restaurant, and read in the lounge until train time at midnight.

We were assured that we had a private compartment, even though it had four bunks. I was so weary that I left my shoes on the floor and climbed up to the bunk, one that the chart said we would occupy.

Pete took one of the lowers. I pulled the covers up and slept through the night. Never heard a thing, and was I surprised to discover the next morning that we had acquired two cabin mates! Man alive was I ever glad to be fully clothed! Pete was awake too, so as quietly as possible we slipped out and went to the dining car for breakfast. So much for the guarantee of privacy. We ate slowly in case they needed time to dress and wash up.

Sure enough, when we returned our fellow travelers were up and looking fresh and clean. We exchanged greetings, and they left for breakfast. It was Good Friday. We had our usual prayer for the family, our mission, and the world. I was just finishing reading the Good Friday scripture in my little Gideon *New Testament* when they returned. The two men sat quietly on the opposite bunk and listened.

The older of the two didn't speak a word of English, so he excused himself and went to join friends in another compartment. Fan Wei Dung, spoke flawless English and was a good-looking young man. After the usual pleasantries, I asked, "Do you know the story I was reading when you came in?"

"No," he answered.

"Have you ever heard of Jesus?" I persisted.

"No, I haven't.

"Easter?" He shook his head, no.

"How about Christmas?"

"No."

"Santa Claus?"

"Oh yes!" He beamed. At last we found common ground.

What followed is hard to explain. Beginning with Santa Claus, a symbol of gift giving, I went from the gift of the Christ Child through Jesus' life, his death as the sacrificial lamb on the cross, burial in the tomb and resurrection on the third day, his forty days with his followers, and his ascension to heaven. The telling took a couple hours, and during that time I didn't have to think about what would come next. It was just there, and it had a life of its own.

Several times Wei Dung slid back the pocket door and looked to see if anyone in the hall was listening. Other than that, he never took his eyes off of mine. It made me feel we were very strongly connected. Pete chose to remain silent. Later he said he spent the time praying.

When I finished, he asked a few questions, then asked to see the book. As he handled it I could see he liked it, so I gave it to him.

"My girlfriend's family has a Bible," he said. "Now I can show her this one. Theirs is much bigger, but it's in Chinese."

"That's wonderful, Wei Dung," I answered. "You can read and study your Bibles together and find a church where you can go to worship and learn more about this wonderful Jesus. I would love to know that you will be his follower too."

"Thank you, thank you," he said as he clasped my gift between his hands. Just seeing him that way made my heart glad.

We spoke of many things in China. "It is much better now than it used to be," he said, "but there is still too much lying. Production and quality reports are never correct. Everybody lies. You can't really trust anyone to be truthful," he said in disgust.

Next I asked about the "one family, one child" law.

"It is hard," he admitted, "but it's important to keep down the population. There's no way to feed so many people."

"That may be true," I answered, "but because each family wants a son to carry on the name, girl babies are aborted and the women keep getting pregnant in the hopes of having a son. The problem is that in twenty years when all these little boys grow up and want brides, there won't be enough to go around, then what do you do?" He seemed concerned about the future for China's young men.

"For years there has been the same problem in Tibet. The custom there is that a woman may take as many as five husbands. Would you like that?"

"Oh no, oh no!" he responded with horror. He had a serious girlfriend and such a prospect was not to his liking. "But it certainly is something to think about." Time has passed, and today it's a serious problem. In North Korea where food is scarce, families are selling their daughters across the border to Chinese farmers. From all accounts, the young girls are willing to go because they will always be able to eat, and their starving families will have money for food too.

Fan Wei Deng and his girlfriend

Wei Dung and his friends got off at a station an hour before we reached Beijing. Before he left he presented me with a small framed picture of himself and his girlfriend, saying, "You gave me a precious gift, so I must give one to you too." He offered it with both hands and a slight nod of the head. I accepted it with both hands and a nod too. I was glad that I knew the custom and could be polite.

We agreed with Molly and Harwood that we'd stay at the Beijing Hotel. They were getting in a day before us and would make reservations. When we reached the hotel and wanted to sign in, there were no reservations for us, and there were no Sturtevants either! We asked them to check all the records. There was nothing. What to do? Pete then asked if any messages had been left for us. Reaching into a drawer they took out a whole bunch of notes and dumped them on the counter. Sorting through them we found two for us. Glory hallelujah! This was a city of eight million souls, and we needed to find my sister. Because their travel agent got a better price at the Xi Yuan, they were staying there. I was glad Pete had the presence of mind to ask.

We got another taxi to the Xi Yuan. Thank heaven they were cheap. At the desk there was no reservation for us but the Sturtevants were there, and there was an empty room adjoining. What a relief! Just as we were finishing checking in, I looked up and saw the back of

Harwood's head way across the huge lobby. I called out his name. Deaf as he was he heard me, and running toward each other, we met halfway.

It took hours to get caught up on families—they had five children, all married and producing grandchildren, and their life in Xian was "interesting."

The two of us with Molly and Harwood

A young friend named Xiaolin (pronounced Shao-lin) was also in town. A year earlier she applied for a student visa to the States. She worked months to meet all the requirements from both the Chinese and U.S. governments, to say nothing of spending a lot of money each step of the way. Many palms needed to be crossed with silver, and the trip to Beijing was costly. When she went to the U.S. consulate she was very badly treated.

The vice-consul flipped through her papers, hardly ever looking at her, all the while in rapt conversation with a German woman off to one side. At the end of her appointment he said, "Maybe I'll give you a visa, and maybe I won't." With that she was dismissed and told to come back in three days. She was devastated.

Hearing that made me so mad that I sat down and wrote a letter to Ambassador Stapelton Roy on hotel stationery, expressing my indignation at the way she was dealt with. I ended the letter by saying we were going to be in town three more days, and should he wish to call, I'd be available. I also enclosed one of our OMS calling cards and a copy of Pete's military ID showing that he was a colonel.

When Xiaolin went for her appointment she was seen by a different officer who said he was pleased to inform her that her visa had been granted. She called us right away to give us the good news.

"Your letter was right on top of my file!" She came over to our hotel to tell us all about it, and in the midst of our conversation the phone rang. It was the consular officer who approved the visa.

"Thank you for writing," he said, and I want to respond to your letter. I know the other officer very well, and he's a fine man who would never act in an inappropriate way (whatever that is). Perhaps Xiaolin was a bit overanxious and didn't understand all he said."

Whatever, I hope that in the future that Mr. JWL will be a bit more kind to his interviewees!

Xiaolin gets her visa

To celebrate we thought we'd go out for Peking duck but found we had waited too long. All such restaurants were closed until 4:00 p.m. We then decided to try the biggest McDonald's in the world that had opened just the day before. Crazy, we never eat at McDonald's, but why not? We drove over there, got our Big Macs and something to drink and found a table. We were no more than seated when a nice-looking man took the table next to us, and we started talking. The reason this was the largest McDonald's in the world is that it has the greatest number of cash registers. On opening day they had 14,000 transactions, so they probably served from 30-35,000 people. It turned out he was the quality-assurance man for Mac Donald's dairy products. He insisted we should try their pineapple sundae, saying it was the best ever; we did and it was. He came from Glenn Ellen, Illinois. He gave us his card

and said if we were ever in the area to give him a call
and he'd show us though "Hamburger University." He
was really taken with Xiolin's cute dimples.

Doing all the touristy things brought back
memories of the days I'd lived there in 1947-1948 and
frequently visited with the many guests who came from
Shanghai. Our son Edwin was five years old and loved
to go along. After hearing the guide's spiel a couple of
times, he could say it by heart and loved to give it with
exactly the same intonations.

In royal robes

When we visited the Summer Palace, Pete and I
decided to do another fun thing. For a couple of dollars
we rented costumes and had our pictures taken. Pete

looked very regal in his emperor's robe and hat, and I felt elegant in the empress dowager's gown.

We had lunch near the marble boat and drank lots of tea before a boat ride across the lake and a long walk back to the front gate. The rest rooms where one pays are pretty good. You buy a ticket for about five cents and receive a double sheet of toilet paper. Next you go to the man at the door. He takes your ticket and lets you in. They are quite clean and not too smelly. The paper is something else though. It is very biodegradable, and when wet turns to mush. Having your own tissues is a very good idea. Anyway, on the day in question, I was in great need of a facility, but the only one I could see was free. By then I couldn't wait any longer and had to go in. Surprise! It was a thirty-foot-long room with "squattie-potties" facing each other in stalls without the benefit of doors. All deposits went into a big pit below. The smell was so overwhelming I didn't want to breathe, but my need was greater than my revulsion. The last stall was unoccupied. I took it and looked around for a place to put my purse where it wouldn't get into anything. A little woman squatting in the opposite stall smiled sweetly and pointed to a peg on the wall. Bless her. Well, there was nothing for it but to do the needful regardless of who saw me. I'd never see any of these folks again, so why worry? The woman across the way just continued to stay there and smiled sweetly at me the whole time. She was precious.

Back in the city in the afternoon we walked to the Dung-An market where I used to shop, but there was nothing I recognized. From there we went the short distance to the street where we used to lived. We were there on Sunday with Molly and Harwood, hoping to celebrate Easter at the Community Church. It had been turned into a residence, subdivided for several families. How blessed they were to be living in a house built for worship. Did they know? Probably not. The numbers had changed, but I recognized what used to be our residence at # 7 Non Ho Yen. It was a really lovely home with a moon door between the living room and dining room, a small moon opening for the fireplace, and an enclosed yard with a pretty "ting-za" (Chinese tea house) with a built-in barbecue. The Christmas when Edwin was five he saw the hot fire burning there and wondered how the dear little Christ Child was going to come down the chimney. I guess he wasn't the first one to get the Christmas stories mixed up.

Beijing is clean of litter and trash, but it surely is dusty. The sky was so yellow that at times we could look right at the sun and not hurt our eyes. Molly and Harwood said that Xian is even worse. I got a beauty of a sinus infection, but fortunately Harwood travels with little baggies of pills for any and every emergency, and he had what I needed. After they left the next day, Pete began to have problems, and my few over-the-counter drugs were of little help. That night on the ferry he coughed so much neither of us slept. I could hardly wait to get him to the 121st Field Hospital at Yongsan in Seoul.

Our return trip back to Korea was easier. We took the train to Tinjing, the seaport for Beijing, and boarded a twenty-four-hour ferry to Inchon. While waiting in the foreigners' lounge, we were delighted to see a group of about fifteen following a little man carrying a yellow Elder Hostel sign mounted on a stick. For years we've supported their work and figured some day we'd take advantage of their offerings.

This ship was much larger than the first one, and we had bunks instead of the floor to sleep on. Sunday, our full day at sea, I was on the stairs after breakfast when I saw a man with a Bible and hymn book in his hand. I asked if there was to be a worship service someplace. He looked startled and answered, "Yes, would you like to come?" I said we would. He introduced himself as the captain of the ship. He asked our room number and said he'd get in touch with us right away. He did and took us to a large, unoccupied stateroom where attendees sat on the floor. They got a chair for Pete because his football knees couldn't take it. A Korean pastor, his wife, and two children, the captain, two businessmen, and the two of us made up the group. It made up for not being able to attend a service on Easter Sunday.

We went through the usual lines when we disembarked and were shown into a large room to wait our turn to get the final checkout. We were near the end of the line and from its slow movement anticipated a long wait. Not so! A kindly officer spotted us, the only Westerners. He came to push our baggage cart ahead and asked us to follow. He took us through a VIP gate, bid us good day and left. That kind of thing happened to us over and over again while we were in Korea.

It was wonderful to be back in the compound again, and in our own bed. Starting May 1 the first batch of guests was due with many to follow that would keep us chasing ourselves for several months.

When I came to the end of transcribing a set of four lectures that Dr. Cho gave in Japan, there were still two or three places where I simply couldn't understand what he said. I played the tape for Dr. Mary Conklin, who would know if he was saying something in Latin, but she couldn't figure them out either. Anne was visiting at the time, and she couldn't even make a guess. I left the spaces blank and asked Mrs. Lee, his administrative manager, to ask him to fill them in so I could finish the work. He was a busy man, but in five minutes he could have provided the missing words, yet somehow I never got the answers. Shortly before we were to be out of country for six months, I went to his office to add a little pressure. I yearned to get them done and in his hands before we left. The reception room was full of people waiting to see Dr. Cho. He was in a private meeting and not to be interrupted. When he finally opened the door, he came straight to me and gave me a hug, which is quite unusual. Knowing he had a lot of others wanting to talk to him, I cut to the chase.

"Dr. Cho," I said, patting his forearm as we shook hands, "be a good boy, now and take fifteen minutes to fill in the blanks, please?" There was an audible gasp at my remark, and I knew the others in the room were shocked that I should speak in such a way to the president. Turning to them and pointing to my white hair I said with a smile, "I can say that because of this." They relaxed and laughed. Age has its privilege in Korea.

May of 1992 was one hectic month. For two weeks the OMS field leaders from all over the globe and headquarters personnel came for four days of intensive meetings, followed by members of the board of trustees and their wives for the first-ever board meeting on one of the foreign fields.

Those first days were the hardest. There were all-day meetings, and they were held in our family room.

Three of the men, including Gery, stayed with us, so we gave them breakfast. The meetings began at 8:00 a.m. We provided a coffee break at 10:00, lunch at 12:00, an afternoon refreshment break at 4:00, and dinner at 6:30. All this for thirty-two people. The other women on the compound and I were busy from morning to well into the night preparing ahead, serving, and cleaning up. For two dinners we went to Yong San, but even that required getting permission from the provost marshall's office to take them in and arranging for a restaurant to accommodate the group in one room at a specific time. At the end of the first day I wasn't sure we'd survive, but as we got into the routine it was a piece of cake.

When the board arrived, the group numbered sixty-five. That was more than we could accommodate, so all meetings were held at the Lotte Hotel or at OMS offices. It was a lot of people to keep track of and move around in a timely fashion. Saturday two special buses were booked to take them to the DMZ, but they had to have breakfast first. In order to keep on schedule and not lose anyone, JB asked us to get carryout breakfasts from Burger King on base and deliver them to the Lote Hotel parking lot. That was one of the easiest things of the week because the manager was terrific. Instead of finding such an order a problem, he thanked us again and again for giving them the business. Pickup time was 6:30 a.m. He got his staff there early to fill our order.

It was ready to go when we arrived. The breakfast of egg-and-bacon croissant, orange juice, and coffee came to about $2.50 each; the croissants and coffee were hot and the juice was cold. The hotel breakfast was $14. It was a hefty saving for the guests. Another morning they went to a dawn prayer meeting at 4:00 a.m., and we made arrangements for breakfast at the golf club on base.

When they got back from the DMZ several of us met them at I'Taewan to help them shop. That was a circus! Two or three at a time is easy, but sixty-five? The best we could do was to have as a meeting place the wide space on the sidewalk in front of McDonalds for anyone who needed help. Their enthusiasm was wonderful, and all came away with loads of treasure for themselves, their children, and grandchildren. Once they had a taste of shopping, they were ready for more any time there was a free hour or two.

The purpose of having the meetings here was that J.B. Crouse, the new president of OMS, felt it was absolutely necessary to make some big changes in the board and in his line of authority if he was to be an effective leader. He wanted them here, away from the usual distractions at home, and he wanted them to see the Christian impact on this country. There were long, tough meetings in which things were hammered out, in spite of quite a bit of opposition on some points. But he had done his homework and was a very persuasive man.

Two major things were accomplished. The first was a partnership agreement between OMS and the Korean Evangelical Holiness Church (KEHC) whereby the two would be equal partners in world evangelization. Other less-developed fields were to work toward that goal as opportunity arose. The second was the inauguration of JB as president of OMS. After his thirty-four years in Korea and the new partnership agreement just signed, it was fitting that it should be held in Seoul. It was a beautiful service.

Within two days all but a couple of the guests had left, beds were stripped and remade, laundry done, and we were ready for the next batch of guests. It was hard to believe that an event we worked on for so long was over, done, finished! Time marches on.

Right after the OMS board members departed, the Adventures in English (AIE) people arrived. One of their first nights in country I had twelve for a steak dinner. The next morning we had a meeting of all staff, American and Korean, followed by luncheon for twenty—there was a lot of cooking to do. I was pleased that the Air Force Korea Network, (AFKN) had such programs as "Sixty Minutes" and "Murder, She Wrote" to enjoy as I worked.

On the 4th of July we took 28 AIE and OMSers to the base and thoroughly enjoyed the celebration. The Republic of Korea (ROK) honor guard gave a spectacular demonstration of a silent drill such as the marines put on, but it was much bigger and used about a hundred men. That was followed by a band concert, and the evening ended with one of the best fireworks shows I've ever seen. There were beautiful bursts of light and showers of rockets going off right over our heads about fifty feet in the air. Later in the week we got in a little culture, spending an evening with the Roger Wagner Chorale, a very special treat. Toward the end of their program they sang a couple of numbers in Korean. It brought the house down.

One of the things I especially enjoyed was showing guests what Seoul looked like at night. We could drive most of the way up the hill I walked in the mornings; then we walked the rest of the way. The view from the top was spectacular.

Korea is known for its huge churches—the largest church in the world, the largest Presbyterian and Methodist churches in the world, but even more impressive are the hundreds of thousands of small ones. Wherever there are a few believers, they form a church. Sometimes it's in a home, or they might rent a few rooms or a floor of a commercial building. Whatever they could afford, they let it be known that it was a church by putting a red neon cross on the roof. From the top of the mountain Seoul looked like a sea of red crosses.

Pete and I were privileged to meet many wonderful people in Korea, but there are two very special young men and their wives with whom we've been able to keep in contact. We met both of them at the very first English for Ministry and Missions (EMM) conference.

On first evening of the two-week program, we stood in a large circle. Trudy started by giving her name, followed by the next person giving his name and his wife's. It continued for about thirty people, so when it got to us we knew all the names and faces. Fortunately the Koreans gave their Christian names.

Johnny Song introduced himself by saying, "Heeeer's Johnny," just like the introduction to Johnny Carson's show. How could we forget his name? Farther on Jacob Jin gave his name, and all the others before him. He was shy but had a sparkle in his eyes. I immediately connected him with a ladder, Jacob's ladder. Later that evening I asked him, "Jacob, where is your ladder?" At first he had no idea what I meant and was perplexed by my question. As time passed we had further contact with both of them and grew aware of what outstanding people they were. The Lord had his hand on them for something special.

Their first experience with missions came when they were with a group of eight on a summer tour through several Southeast Asian countries, living with the inhabitants and sharing the gospel. Johnny, Jacob, and Joshua needed financial assistance; Pete provided it at a hundred dollars apiece. Additionally we bought them sleeping bags and other essentials. We called them our three Js. They said, no, they were four Js because Jesus was going with them. They were on the road for six weeks and had every kind of experience from acceptance and thanks to utter rejection. It was a real eye-opener for three aspiring missionaries.

Johnny graduated from seminary, married Hannah, a lovely girl who had a degree in hospital administration, and heard a call to reach out to the Muslims. He joined Operation Mobilization (OM) and went to England for his initial training and ministry. Later he went to Turkey and worked with the Kurds. At one time he was arrested for handing out Christian literature and spent a few weeks in jail. He wrote of his experience, and immediately we responded with, "Johnny, what good company you're keeping, Peter, Paul, and all the rest!

Several years and two children later (Jane and Chan Ho), his focus changed. After a lot of prayer and investigation, he had a call to start a school for young people preparing for foreign missions. Land and buildings became available in New Zealand. He raised the money to rent it and later bought it for a training center. He called it the Intercultural Institute of New Zealand. To date most of the students are from Korea, but in time they hope to attract others from all over the Far East, the United States, and Europe. For effective outreach, a good command of English is a must as well as cross-cultural skills.

Before students arrived, they already had a sponsoring organization to which they went when they finished their programs. They came individually or several in a group. The institute was still growing and changing, and with the help of several excellent educators, Johnny was building a fine, accredited school.

Jacob had quite a story. Born into a very poor family, he lost his father when he was young. His mother worked at the lowly job of cleaning bathhouses and couldn't earn enough to keep all her children with her. In order to survive she put Jacob and a brother in an orphanage for several years. To this day it's a very painful memory. But the Lord can use that too.

He passed the entrance examination to STU, but there still wasn't enough money. He was given a scholarship and earned a room in the attic of the chapel by keeping the building clean. The women on the food line in the dining hall saved him bowls of rice and side dishes. The professors liked him, and when his clothes got a little ragged and worn, they bought him new ones. Getting Jacob through college and seminary was a community effort.

While still in seminary Jacob married Lucy. Pete and I were honored to attend their wedding, as we had Johnny and Hannah's. It's a Korean custom that when the bride is walking to join her groom, it's very bad luck if either of them smiles. That didn't apply to them—they were both beaming, and if being lucky had anything to do with having sons, they were very lucky with three beautiful boys.

During our last year with OMS, Jacob called me every Saturday night. The conversation always began with, "Grandmother, I am Jacob." He usually had something interesting to report.

"Grandmother, Lucy and I have the same characteristic," he said one time.

"What do you mean?" I asked.

"Both very stubborn," he answered.

"What did you do about it, Jacob?" I guessed they must have had their first big fight.

"Lucy cried and I prayed." That was so like him.

"Grandmother, we have fruit," he announced on another call.

That's wonderful, Jacob. What kind of fruit did you buy?"

"You don't understand," he said. "Lucy's pregnant." And so it was that they began their family. I always looked forward to our conversations. When we were leaving Seoul for the last time, Jacob and Lucy couldn't come to the airport because of other commitments. He called just before we left and said, "Grandmother, I will miss your hugs."

Jacob and Lucy applied to the Wycliffe, and were sent to England for training. Now they are in Kunming, China, working with the Black Meao tribe so they can translate the Bible into their language. We are so proud of them. Years earlier Jacob said his goal was to establish a seminary in China; and if some day he fulfills that dream, it wouldn't surprise me in the least.

In July came the big mission effort, the annual two-week AIE seminar. A number of people came from England and the States. Pete and I decided we'd be gofers, and it was good. It was hotter than blue blazes in the afternoons at the seminary. I was one of several who agreed to take a morning Bible class, "Feed My Sheep," based on the Twenty-third Psalm. I didn't look forward to the three hours it took every day, but once we got into it, I loved it.

My group was great. Each student chose a biblical name, some of them quite interesting. There was Grace Lee, Mina Gill, wife of a pastor whose daughter was already in the States; Salvation Lee, a missionary returning to Saipan and in Korea to find a wife; Paul Kim; Timothy Jung; Silas Ryong; and Shadow Cho. Shadow chose her name because she said she lives in the shadow of the Almighty. For me it was a wonderful experience.

Cross-cultural skills are very important, and we introduced them often. For a scheduled Indian dinner, I got the makings and with the help of the Korean staff cooked an Indian curry dinner for 130 people. The only thing I had to do was make the banana chutney the day before and bring all the spices for the curry and the potatoes. They provided the chicken and rice. The cooks didn't like one little bit having anyone invade their territory, and I was only reluctantly accepted inside their doors. I had a time getting them to cook the curry my way. They were sure that it was best to boil the chicken and then put the sauce over it. Mina Gill was helping me, so I knew there was no misunderstanding, but it took a lot of time to get them to cook the chicken *in* the sauce. I told them how many onions were needed. They had them ready to chop, but after doing only half, they decided that was enough and put the rest away. I gave the amount of garlic needed; they dumped in about four times that amount, and thus it went. Even so it turned out very well. Pete went to an Indian restaurant in I'Taewan and picked up *nan* (bread) to go with the dinner. The Indian guest who was speaking that night gave us high praise for the dinner, but I suspect he was being kind.

A big part of having the Indian meal was to help students accept other cultures. They were given no utensils, and for some it was disgusting to eat with their fingers (right hand only) and not use chopsticks and spoons.

During our last AIE I was very careful to be with Pete wherever he went, and we held hands, particularly when walking from one building to the other. His sight was by then so poor it would have been easy for him to stumble. There were other married people on staff, but we were the only couple. Soon the students began calling us "the young couple."

Seana Staley, Pete's granddaughter, came out to take a special summer term at Yunsei University for Koreans born and brought up outside of Korea, and those adopted as infants. The course was founded to help people like her appreciate and enjoy their native heritage. After a week-long bus tour to major points of interest, she signed up for two classes for which she got full college credit. She had no classes on Wednesdays and could spend the day with us. Saturdays and Sundays were also free. She had a good bit of studying to do and was faithful about doing it. One of her courses required a lot of reading, about 150 pages a day! Seana learned her way around I'Taewan and did some shopping but was anxious for her mother, Bonnie, to arrive at the end of the month before getting into any serious stuff.

In mid-July Bonnie, after graduating from Indiana Wesleyan and moving to Washington, D.C., for a new job, came for a visit, The time went all too quickly. She and Seana departed for home August 9, giving little time to catch our breath before packing up and moving into the Crouses' house next door, making "Petersons' Pad" available for rental. Since JB was president of OMS, he and Bette moved to headquarters in Greenwood, Indiana.

We departed Seoul September 13, nonstop to Chicago. Anne met us and took us to their house in Greenwood. She and Gery left Hong Kong after five years. He was named vice-president for Homeland Ministries of OMS at headquarters. We bought a car and proceeded to make the rounds, visiting family and checking up on friends on the way home to Florida. We looked back on the years in Korea with thanksgiving for the opportunities for service as "honorary missionaries." There's nothing better.

NB
A Tribute to Col. and Mrs. Conrad R. Peterson

Pete, better known as Colonel Saint Pete, and his wonderful wife, Fran, were a terrific answer to prayer for the OMS work in Korea. We had been praying for a special couple who had just the right gifts to fit our job description of host and hostess, public relations, and to assist with our English ministries. God had just the right couple in mind that had been prepared to fit the bill perfectly.

Colonel Saint Pete had a lifetime of serving overseas with the U.S Air Force and ministering cross-culturally. Fran was born of missionary parents in what is now North Korea and was right at home with culture and language. What a special couple they were and so gifted to fill the bill and be an outstanding host and hostess for the Korea field.

They met airplanes, made trips to Panmunjun, shepherded guests on sight-seeing tours around the city, took them to see the seminary, the churches, and to I'Taewon, the famous shopping market in Seoul, and gave everybody a sixty-four-dollar tour of what God is doing in Korea.

Fran is a wonderful cook, and guests had many delicious meals around the table.

At our weekly Thursday-night prayer meetings they were always such a vital part of our team. We appreciated Fran and Pete sharing their testimonies, prayer requests, and spiritual insights. We all enjoyed so much listening to Pete's deep bass voice.

We at OMS are so grateful for the five years of outstanding service they contributed to the work in Korea from 1988-1992. Pete and Fran, thank you for answering the call. We thank God for the body of Christ, the gift of friendship and rich memories we have of our days together with you in Korea, and praise God for the tremendous contribution you made to His kingdom in that land.

J.B Crouse, Jr.
President Emeritus

We believe that Col. Saint Pete and Fran were a gift to the OMS family in Korea right out of God's plan book. They brought with them encouragement, caring, joy, laughter, prayer, compassion, and listening ears. They endeared themselves to us as a missionary family living on campus in so many ways. We celebrated together, we prayed together, and we worked together. We had ministries that brought us together in faith and responsibility. Pete and Fran not only endeared themselves to us as a mission family but also to every visitor who came. Their gracious hospitality made visits of people from around the world memorable times. Fran and Pete had stories to tell that people carried away with them in their hearts. We always enjoyed Fran's creative plans for celebration. We continue to be thankful to the Lord for the memories that we have of those days together enriched by deep-hearted friendship with Fran and Pete. We love them and are better because they journeyed with us in our walk of obedience to the Lord.

> By God's Grace and for His Glory
> Bette Shipps Crouse
> Assistant to the President

Home Again in Satellite Beach 1993

We were home in time to be involved in preparation for Christmas festivities. The choir was already rehearsing "Joy, the Gift of Christmas." Fortunately we were provided tapes for our parts. I played mine while cooking and cleaning up to the point where Pete lost patience.

"If you don't quit playing those tapes all the time I'll be singing alto too!" he said. He didn't need any extra help for his bass part.

We reserved Wednesday evenings for the many church activities that began with a family dinner. Without a regular kitchen staff, several of us agreed to take one Wednesday a month; and we signed up for the fourth. Ours was to be chicken. We got fried chicken one night from Albertson's, but it turned out to be just dreadful—heavy, fat-soaked breading and dry meat inside. After that we did it ourselves. We bought bags of leg quarters for twenty-eight cents a pound and an equal quantity of breasts. After cutting away all the skin and extra fat, we first dipped them in plain yogurt then seasoned bread crumbs and baked them. Tender? They were out of this world. Friends did baked potatoes for us and brought them in; others came early and put together a huge tossed salad. On the day before, I made several fresh apple cakes to be served with whipped cream. A good meal, and we brought it in for under two dollars apiece for adults, a dollar for the young people, and children under twelve, free. The first time we served 60 but word soon got around jumping the number to 120.

We planned to go to Arlington for Easter with Bonnie, who had moved there from Indiana. With her degree in hand she got a good job with Green Thumb, a not-for-profit organization devoted to aiding seniors in the work force.

Pete complained of indefinable aches and pains, that nothing seemed to help. When it got bad enough for a serious look he was put in the hospital right away. On Palm Sunday morning a very rotten gall bladder was removed. Fortunately they did it with four little holes that healed up quickly, and there was a minimum of discomfort. Diane Weber came to sit with me during the operation. I was so thankful for her company, particularly when the doctor came to announce that had we waited another day, it would have ruptured, and Pete would have died! That was a shocker and took my breath away, but just to be sure about his information, I called my doctor brother-in-law, Harwood Sturtevant. Whenever there were medical questions, I ran them by him.

"Yes, indeed, had it burst Pete couldn't have survived," he said. It was too close for comfort, and we praised the Lord for good doctors who know their business.

In May the General Assembly of the Presbyterian Church, USA, met in Orlando, a boon for all of us in the area. We signed up as volunteers. Pete was assigned to the information booth to help register 7,500 "observers" and answer questions, mostly about where telephones and restrooms could be found. I worked in the hospitality room, as an usher, and in the gift shop. We both sang in the choir of one thousand voices and sat in on as many meetings as we could. The hotel next door charged only twenty dollars a night for us "worker bees," making it no strain on the budget.

At the OMS Conference in the early summer we met a few who had visited Korea while we were there, making it much like old home week.

"Are you the one who took my husband shopping when he was in Korea," a woman asked, beaming. "I just want to thank you so much for showing him this beautiful eel-skin bag. I absolutely love it! Thank you, thank you!" Quite often I pressed the men to try shopping in I'Taewan.

"How can you go home empty-handed," I asked. "You've been in Korea and didn't buy anything for your wife or grandchildren? Impossible!" Reluctantly, they gave in and then were very pleased with what they could present to their families. It was a good feeling.

Pete's eyes deteriorated to the point where he gave up golf except when we could go out together, usually late in the afternoon when there was still enough light for nine holes. I stood behind him and could see exactly where the ball went, but if he got into the rough I had to find it. Never mind, it was a good time of day to be walking the course, and quite often we met young airmen having a round. We joined up to make a foursome. That was super because their young eyes could always find what I missed.

The End of the Road 1994 - 2001

Going back to Korea each summer was a joy. The first mornings of climbing the hill above the compound again was such fun. I was warmly greeted. We exchanged high fives, and the elderly women insisted I should not leave again. I joined them for greetings and a little conversation. Sometimes we sang together. Often Korean women stood next to the monument, and in trying to relieve the pain in their hips or back, bumped them repeatedly against the stone.

"Aren't you afraid you'll knock it down if you keep bumping it that way," I asked?

"Oh no," came a laughing response, "it's really very strong."

Each year the AIE program was better than before. Pete and I carried a light load and always worked together except for two of the electives. I helped students put out a newspaper each week, and Pete worked with Carol Mitchell to teach barbershop singing.

One year we stayed in the Sandoz house while they were on leave and had four of the volunteers with us on weekends. One was Christine Lytle, a college senior. She kept us laughing as she told stories about her students. One day she asked her conversation class to bring pictures of themselves and families to share. She had pictures of herself also, one of them taken several months before when her hair was short and curly. She had since let it grow.

"Your hair is no longer curly," one of the girls observed.

"When it grew out it was straight," Christine answered.

"Oh, you have magic hair!"

They also asked about her personal life. Korean students aren't in the least hesitant to do so. It's not considered improper.

"Do you have a fiancé?" one inquired.

"No, I don't."

" Do you have a boyfriend?" she persisted,

"No," Christine said.

"Do you not have the ability?" she pressed. By this time we were double over with laughter. Christine was having quite an education in cross-cultural skills.

Each time we came to the wrap-up of a seminar, we were thankful for the rich opportunity to live and work with dedicated people in such a good cause.

Our friend Anne Campbell came twice and held a Bible class or two in her Baptist church, she enjoyed the give-and-take with the Korean students. On one of her first days during a relaxed time of getting to know them, she was talking with an older man.

"Have you ever been in Korea before?" he asked.

"This is my first time," she answered, "but my husband served here in the Korean War."

"He came and served here? I stand in honor of your husband," he said as he came to his feet, tears streaming down his face.

Gertrude Bryan

Gertrude was the stepmother of my first husband, Kedar Bryan. When I married Pete she was pleased to have a new son-in-law and immediately accepted him as part of the family. Kedar's sister, Alice Hondru, did as well. It was a very happy thing for me. She even provided the wedding cake. Every time we went to Washington to visit Bonnie, we made it a point to have plenty of time for Mother, then living a few blocks away in Goodwin House. She loved to dine out, and being driven around in Pete's big Lincoln made her feel like the Queen of the May. She particularly liked the Ft. Myers Officers Club. Before each trip I told her to make a list of things we could do for her.

As years passed and she was less and less able to get around, we took her shopping. Without fail, she needed shoes, available only at a particular store in Shirlington. Department stores simply don't have the personnel to serve a customer with Mother's needs. When we took her to a swanky dress shop in Alexandria she'd heard about, she was in clover. The clerks were attentive, the selection was perfect, and the dressing room was large enough for the wheelchair, two helpers and me. She came away loaded.

Mother had a new request: she wanted to buy a special all-in-one undergarment and knew exactly where the store was in downtown Washington. She'd been there before. It was the only place in the whole metropolitan area that had it. Fine. I'd done a lot of shopping in the area during the 1950s, and I knew where the place was. Oh how things had changed! One-way streets, all kinds of construction going on, nothing looked familiar—and it was pouring rain. I got as close as I could to the door, and unloaded her in a No Parking zone. Pete took her in while I went to park the car.

When I got there she was already in one of the dressing rooms being fitted. Mother was one hundred years old, and nature has a way of shifting things around.

There was a lot of tucking and fixing before they took the garment to be altered. Mother felt embarrassed at being so helpless. The two black saleswomen were full of humor and good cheer, though, and didn't let anything discourage them.

"You is still breathin' ain't ya?" "You should praise de Lawd." "You is still up and around, ain't ya, so praise de Lawd." By this time we were all laughing, and even Mother saw some humor in it. Out in the waiting room, Pete wondered what all the hilarity was about. We waited with him while the alterations were made. She paid the bill, but when they brought the garment nicely wrapped up she said, "Oh no, I want to wear it." Back she went to the dressing room for another round of pulling, tugging, and laughing. Pete said he had no idea that putting on a new girdle could be such fun. Those two little ladies were priceless.

We got back to Goodwin House at lunchtime. She always liked to have us escort her to the dining room. I suggested she put in her lower denture before we went down.

"I don't have it," she said. Mother's mind was always as sharp as a tack, but in the last year she had some interesting tales.

"Last week," she told us, "I went to a beautiful dinner-dance in the most elegant ballroom. It was wonderful to watch everybody, lighthearted and gay as they swirled around the floor. It reminded me so much of our early days in Shanghai. When the dancing stopped, the master of ceremonies came up to me and held out his hand. "Give me your teeth," he said. "I took them

out and gave them to him, and I haven't seen them since."
She said all this with a perfectly straight face; obviously
she believed it. The next time we were at the nurse's
station Pete asked if they had heard of this great event.
They had.

On our previous visit Mother complained that her
dentures hurt, and when we suggested she get them
checked by the dentist, she said something about its
being too hard to get over to see him and impossible to
get an appointment. We knew she had plenty of money
to take care of all her needs and that Goodwin House
would provide transportation. Apparently she just didn't
want to bother with it. We began to speculate what she
might have done with the denture. She could easily have
flushed it down the toilet or dropped it in a wastebasket
where it wouldn't be noticed. It was simply not to be
found.

Each time we visited, I routinely went through
her clothes. Some needed to be dry-cleaned and went in
one pile. Another was for things to send to the thrift
shop, and still others needed to be spot-cleaned before
washing. I checked the pockets as I went, and what do
you know—there were her teeth! She was so surprised
to see them again. Without hesitation asked me to wash
them, and she popped them into her mouth!

She celebrated her one hundredth birthday
joyously with family and friends. We were on hand for
her hundred and first, but her days were less and less

fulfilling and more of a burden. She was a take-charge person with a wide circle of friends and many interests. With her being reduced to constant care and limitations, we didn't wish her many more years. On December 6, 1997, while talking with Anne on the phone and another granddaughter, Robyn, at her side, she slipped into glory. God is good all the time.

Gertrude Bryan

In early March of 1996 Pete had a really bad bellyache. He never complained, but when he did I hustled him off to the doctor. He had to have bilateral-hernia surgery, so the doctor put a nice big smile across his lower abdomen and did the job.

"You can take him home this afternoon," the doctor announced.

"Not on your life," I told him. "The man has problems, and I don't want him for at least twenty-four hours. You keep him." The next day was soon enough. We had an appointment to see the surgeon in three days, and were surprised that he took the stitches out so soon. Later in the day while he was resting and I was in the den, Pete called me. "Honey come look at this. There is blood all over the place." A spot about an inch and a half long had opened up and was bleeding profusely! I handed him a clean towel to hold over the wound, pressing as hard as was comfortable, and we hurried back to be stitched up again. The doctor was lucky we weren't the sort to sue at the drop of a hat.

That was also the year of Pete's eightieth surprise birthday party in Arlington. Bonnie put on a big bash for her dad. When Denny, his younger brother from Seattle, showed up the night before at a big Chinese dinner, Pete knew it wouldn't be an ordinary affair. Friends, family, and fellow servicemen from all over came to celebrate his life and friendship. What a treat to see how much they loved him, my man. Standing next to him I was the most blessed of all.

With Bonnie at Pete's 80th birthday celebration

On March 2, 1997, Pete and I attended a couple's retreat in Cocoa Beach. We had afternoon and evening meetings followed by a walk on the beach and time alone. Sunday morning began with breakfast in the lounge. Just as we were getting our coffee, we were called to come to the conference room. We thought perhaps they wanted us to participate in some way. Michael Carey, our pastor, came up to me and said, "Fran, your son Jim has died."

"Jimmy, my baby?" I gasped. "How did it happen?"

"He died of a heart attack last night. Donna has been trying to reach you and finally traced you down through the church this morning." I was stunned and overcome with the enormity of the loss. Jimmy, that funny little guy who filled my life with such joy and laughter, who nearly drove me crazy when he was a teenager but became such a wonderful man—husband, father, and son. How was I going to live without him? Why, Lord? Why did you have to take him away? There were no answers, just a great big hole in my heart, and floods of tears.

My sons, Edwin and Jim

Pete and I flew to Minneapolis the next day. As we circled the airport I remembered feeling, I didn't want the plane to land. As long as we were up there, Jim's death wasn't real. On the ground it would be. We landed.

Anne and Gery drove from Billings, picking up granddaughter Lisa and her baby son on the way. Having them there, the joy and comfort of their presence was pure blessing, but nothing eased that awful pain in my chest. My baby, my little Jimmy-boy was gone, gone forever. Why, Lord, oh why? Pete was like a rock. His arms held me tight, and he didn't try to say anything. He just held me. Bonnie came. She and Anne were as close as sisters and blessed each other.

Donna's mother and dad were there, and Donna was amazing. Hers was the greatest loss as was Christian's, but she was holding it all together, and Christian didn't even seem to notice. I had walked in her shoes and knew she was running on energy that was not her own, but a "given" for such times as those.

Gery, who was to conduct the service the next day, had us sit around a table and talk about Jim. We told stories of the good, the noble, and the funny things he did. It was salve to my wounded heart and the beginning of the healing process.

At the funeral service the next day the place was packed with his friends from the plant where he worked and dozens of Christian's friends from school.

Bonnie sang "On Eagle's Wings," which brought another flood of tears. I didn't want him borne away on eagle's wings! I wanted him here, Lord. Why did you take him away?

Gery conducted a wonderful, thoughtful service, reminding us again of how fragile and precious life is, but we never know which day or how we will be called home.

Mike, Jim's boss, spoke, and it was good to hear about the part of his life we didn't know so well. He gave both sides of Jim's day at Advanced Circuit Incorporated (ACI). "Jim had little patience with foot-dragging," he said, "When the status quo needed to be changed, he stepped on many toes, but he was right. He took his branch of the manufacturing of sophisticated multilayered printed circuit boards from an unacceptably high level of scrap to almost zero! It resulted in great bonuses for the workers and a deep sense of satisfaction for a job well done. Likewise, Jim was responsible for a change in one of the processes, eliminating the use of a huge tank of hydrogen chloride, a potentially serious risk not only to the plant but to the whole town."

I stood in line with others to greet people as they left. When I introduced myself as Jim's mom, many broke down and wept, hugging me and telling me how they admired and loved him and how much he'd be missed. Yes, my son Jim was a good man.

Most of the family had to leave on Thursday, but Pete and I stayed until Saturday noon. That gave us time to visit the ACI plant on Friday. I really wanted to see where he had worked and have a better feel for his environment. It was comforting to talk with staff and hear how well they liked him. He was the only supervisor who spent little time in his office but was constantly walking the floor. The reason Jim was so successful in making the process work was that he demanded a constant check on the chemical balance, temperatures, and other crucial factors.

When we stopped to see one of the ovens used in the process, the man tending it said Jim asked him to check on temperature variations not only in the center but at the corners of the unit.

"I've had no problem with it," I answered. "It's constant and electrically controlled, so we just leave it alone."

"Humor me," Jim said. "I checked and found there were great variations not only over time but in several parts of the oven." We'll miss Jim big time.

As we were leaving, one of the office staff came running after us, waving papers.

"We did it! we did it!" he shouted. "The rejects this week are a .01%." Everybody clapped and cheered. Yes, my son Jim did that.

There was nothing for it but to try to go on from there. I started crying at most inappropriate times, but I didn't worry about it. I was a grieving mother and had the right. One day the chorus of a hymn kept going through my head, "For I know whate're befalls me, Jesus doeth all things well." I was thankful for the message. Surely God is good.

A little over a year after Jim died, Donna also died of a massive heart attack while mowing the front lawn. She was born with congenital heart defect and underwent four major operations to correct it. For years she was fine; but apparently it didn't stay fixed, and she went very suddenly. She must have suspected something wasn't right, because she wrote a letter to their son, Christian, telling him how much she loved him, and giving instructions about what to do if she wasn't there for him. It was such a shock, particularly for Christian. He was nineteen and a sophomore at Johnson and Wales in Rhode Island. Once again Gery and Anne drove from Billings to be with the family and conduct the service. I flew in from Florida, and Bonnie and Seana came from Washington.

During all their years together, Jim and Donna invested in fine things, mostly from the Orient. When I walked into their home with both of them gone, the house had lost its luster, and all of the treasures were just stuff.

Mary Condon, Donna's best friend and next-door neighbor, invited us to stay with her. All of us pitched in to do what we could to sort things out for Christian. Bonnie went through papers and put aside those he would need to settle his affairs.

On Donna's desk was the letter. In part it said: "Son, you have been my life, my pride, joy, and job. I know I haven't been the most perfect mother (not even close), but know I loved you more than life itself. You've brought such happiness into my life. I'm so glad God gave you to us to care for. I only wish I could see my grandchildren. I love you so much that it hurts to know that I'm no longer here on this earth to be there for you. I will be with my Lord, and hopefully a guardian angel for you. I must go now. I'm sure there is much more to tell you, but the most important has been said, and again, I love you. Take care, and may God bless you. Mom."

I gathered Donna's magazines and cancelled the subscriptions. Dorothy, Donna's mother, went through her personal things, but her wedding and engagement ring set, her pearls, and several pieces of jewelry were missing. They were nowhere to be found. While we were having a light lunch, Dorothy mentioned it, and Mary had the answer.

"Donna said she always put her rings and best

jewelry in the rice to keep them safe."

"In the rice? What do you mean?" Dorothy asked.

"Jim and Donna ate more rice than potatoes and have a big jar of it in the pantry." Mary said. Dorothy dug around in it and sure enough, found a plastic bag containing the missing jewelry.

On a trip to Korea for another AIE, we drove across the country via the southern route, stopping along the way to visit family and friends, ending up with Pete's brother, Denny, in Seattle. We arrived in time to put our names down for space-available travel to Korea and got a flight that put us into Seoul in plenty of time to take part in the orientation. What a good trip, and it cost us all of six dollars apiece! That's my kind of travel. On our return trip we had to go commercial in order to get to Billings in time for a Helsby family gathering. We drove home across the northern tier of states then down the coast to Florida.

It seemed to be the era when the grandchildren were producing their young for the next generation, and the older ones were leaving. Over the preceeding few years many of our families had left us. My brother Jim, the youngest man in the family, went first with a massive heart attack on January 15, 1982; Nathan was next on May 29, 1984, also with heart failure. Hunkey (Cordelia) died in August 1988. Willard seemed very frail during our reunion in late September 1997 and died on October 27. That left Heydon, the oldest of the eight, and the three youngest girls. Men sure are fragile creatures. Add to them my first husband, Kedar Bryan, and our sons Edwin and Jim. The list was growing longer and longer, and all of their deaths except Edwin's were tobacco related! What a terrible cost paid for smoking!

One fall Pete, Bonnie, and I had a ten-day tour of Israel with the Brevard Choral Society. Pete was one of the nonsingers. He said his job was to carry music. We had opportunity to perform several times, and what a treat to sing where the acoustics were perfect. On a Sunday we sang "One Bread, One Body" during Mass at the Church of the Annunciation. Following the service we visited a church built over the place where Mary drew water from a well. A baptism was in progress, and it was noisy. A couple of priests, standing next to an oval tin tub (like one we used to boil clothes in) on a small table, wore aprons over their robes. The infant girl was screaming her lungs out as she was dunked several times and then held up while the sign of the cross was made on her hands, feet, head, and chest. Next she was put back in the tub, and generous amounts of water were poured over her head. After that she was lifted high for everyone to see the newly baptized Christian. At last she was given to her mother who waited with a pink blanket. Two little boys of about three and four were next, and they fought with all their might to hang on to their mothers. They were pulled to the sacrament, kicking and screaming. We didn't stay to watch. It seemed too cruel.

Concerts scheduled in the Dormitian Abbey and the chapel of the Bethlehem University were packed. What a thrill it was to sing in such ancient and hallowed places, and when we sang the finale, a glorious arrangement of "Joy to the World," to see everybody rise clapping and cheering. It was almost too much to bear. At the Church of St. Anne and several others we gathered in the front and sang "The Lord Bless You and Keep You." It was so simple and so beautiful with Pete's wonderful bass voice.

1999 was a mixed bag. Most of it was good, but there were a few difficult days while doctors tried to find out why Pete had serious chest pains and shortness of breath. It happened early one morning, so I whisked him off to the emergency room. For eight days they ran every sort of test and could find nothing wrong. That was encouraging, but what do we do if it happened again? The cause turned out to be overmedication with Synthroid. It was corrected and he was fine. Thank God!

After sixty-two rejections and years of trying to find a publisher for *Journal of the Third Daughter*, I bit the bullet and found Four Seasons Publishers, who would do it for me. It felt so good to hold the finished product in my hand. Promoting it has been demanding, but letters from scores of happy readers are reward enough. Work on the sequel, *A Tale of Two Bamboos,* progressed nicely. If only there were more hours in the day for writing.

Sadly, Anne and Gery Helsby were not able to resolve problems accumulated over the years and were divorced in June, 2000.

Dave and Becky asked us to celebrate Christmas with them. The evening of our arrival we had dreadful headaches, probably because of going from sea level to 4,500 feet in one day. The remedy was to drink water, lots of water! The next morning I was fine, but Pete said he'd been dizzy all night and banged into things when trying to go to the bathroom. I told him to stay in bed, and I'd talk to Becky. Her dad, Bob Long, is a doctor in Taiwan, so what did she do? She called him to ask what Pete needed. He advised a lot of water. Two glasses did the trick, and he was up and ready to go.

He, Anne, and I went out shopping and came back to the house for lunch. With Anne needing to do more, she and I went out again, but Pete stayed home.

While he was telling Dave something about his service days, all of a sudden he couldn't put his thoughts into words. They just didn't connect. He tried to say something to Becky, but nothing worked. Both Dave and Becky realized that something was wrong, and once more she called her dad. His advice was to get Pete to the emergency room immediately! Calling dad in Taiwan was cheaper and faster than consulting a local doctor.

When Anne and I drove in about 5:00 p.m., Becky was out on the deck and waved, telling us to go to the emergency room, that Pete had had a stroke. We went as fast as the law and slippery roads would allow. When we walked in, a nurse pointed the way and said, "He's in there."

By that time Pete was okay. He'd had a TIA. There was no paralysis, and he could even remember everything that happened, including his frustration at not being able to speak. An MRI showed no hemorrhaging or tumor, big relief. But because of his age and being away from his doctors, they decided to keep him overnight and run more tests the next day. That was fine by me. I didn't want responsibility for him in the next few hours.

Becky, bless her heart, brought the kids and a picnic supper to the emergency room. A little nourishment made us all feel better. She then took the family home, and Anne and I stayed until Pete was settled in his private room. The next morning I watched all the tests and loved seeing that little valve jump up every time his heart beat. The final exam was a chest X-ray. They said he was good for at least another twenty years but mustn't neglect to take his aspirin every day.

"I can't thank you enough for the wonderful care you gave both of us," I said to the nurse at the desk as she was checking us out. "We're far from home, and you've done everything perfectly for us. We are most thankful."

"Oh, get out of here or you'll make us cry," the nurses said as they gave us hugs and walked us to the elevator.

Bonny and John Bruetzmacher wedding

The happiest event of the year was Bonnie and John Gruetzmacher's wedding in October—a joyful affair with lots of friends and family present. Pete and Clay both walked her down the aisle. Seana was her maid of honor, and I got to be mother of the bride. We were nearly blinded by Bonnie's three-carat diamond.

September 11 will forever define the year 2001. Everything else fades in comparison to the disaster. Praise the Lord, we had no friends or family involved. The message that came to us was the same that was true for me the first Christmas after Kedar died. All through the season the scriptures announced, "Fear not, Fear not, FEAR NOT!"

Anne came to Satellite Beach during her summer break to put on a fantastic bash with a teddy-bear theme for my eightieth birthday, and Bonnie took a week's vacation to give a beautiful party in honor of Pete's eighty-fifth. Time marched on, and we were more aware than ever it's a matter of maintenance, maintenance, maintenance; so we kept up a schedule of exercise and swimming at the fitness center.

"JB showed us the plans for a half-circle of poles from which flags from all the countries where OMS has a mission were to fly. Naturally there would be one for Korea, and I asked how much it would cost. One thousand dollars, came the answer. I had an idea.

"Honey," I said to Pete, "may I have a pole for Korea for my next birthday?"

"Absolutely, if that's what you want," he answered.

The following week we were at the OMS conference in Indiana. There a strong appeal was made for donations for a building in a seminary in Bangalore, South India. An interested party pledged to match all contributions, a tempting offer. Pete had a small insurance policy that had just been sitting there, doing nothing for years. He suggested giving it to celebrate his next birthday. Why not? We both felt our birthdays that year were honored in a special way.

Anne gets her degree

May brought several events we wanted to attend, and fortunately those were the good old days of senior coupons. For seven hundred dollars we could purchase two round-trip tickets to anyplace in the country or four one-way trips. We chose the latter. For the first leg we went from Orlando to Bozeman, Montana, to help Anne celebrate receiving her master's degree in psychology, specializing in children and families. I'm so proud of my girl. The next leg was out to Seattle to see Pete's younger brother, Denny. He hadn't been well, and the brothers had a lot of catching-up to do. Next came a cross-country flight to Providence, Rhode Island, to watch our grandson, Christian Bryan, strut his stuff as he graduated with honors from Johnson & Wales. How I wished Jim and Donna could have been there too. The last leg was back home to Florida.

We celebrated Christmas in Forth Worth with Bonnie and John their first year in Texas. Anne came from Montana to join us.

For years the Trinh family, our Vietnamese "son" and his family, came for a week every Thanksgiving, but after the children reached school age, it was changed to the day after Christmas up to New Year's. On December 26 we headed for home early in the morning and arrived the evening of the 27th, but the Trinhs got there an hour before us. When we pulled in, Becky already had supper on the stove.

253

Before we left home I loaded the freezer with soups and things they especially liked. We were all set. We celebrated the New Year with them and friends at Disney and the next day they headed north. We made up beds with fresh linens, cleaned bathrooms, and put out fresh towels. It felt just like Korea. The Helsby clan arrived that evening with the same number of parents and children.

Becky Helsby was expecting her fourth baby and couldn't accompany David on a six-week exploratory trip to Africa. Hannah, age seven, went with her dad to "test the waters." Now, two years later, the whole family is moving to Tanzania to build an orphanage for three hundred AIDS-orphaned children. In May 2005 they welcomed baby number five into the family.

Over the next few months Pete had a variety of difficulties, but each in turn was managed. In spite of and in between them life seemed quite normal if a little slower. There were no complaints, and he continued to be his sweet old self. But that summer everything "went south" at the same time. On August 27 he graduated to the Church Triumphant.

Col. Conrad R. Peterson, 1916-2002

(In the words of Dr. Phil)
Lord, What Are You Thinkin'?

My beloved is gone, and I'm heartbroken. I feel empty and without hope.

For two years Pete's health steadily declined, but there was always the anticipation that some new drug or new treatment would bring him back to full vigor. Our years together were packed full of adventure serving you at home and abroad, and although we were both in our eighties, we were eager to keep going.

As it became evident that our "going forth" years were over, we still reveled in our life together, having our morning worship after breakfast, reading your word, and praying. You lifted our spirits and made us feel whole. Life was a little slower, but we managed to work out three times a week. When I saw Pete pumping iron and riding the stationary bike, I breathed a prayer of thanks.

Doctor's visits became more frequent, and Pete constantly apologized for taking up so much of my time driving him to appointments, but it was my joy just to be with him. He always wanted to do whatever he could for me, and until his last week at home, he insisted on taking care of the dinner dishes while I watched the evening news followed by Dr. Phil.

One night when I got him into bed, put the drops in his eyes, and removed his hearing aids, he looked up at me and said, "Fran, you are so precious." I needed nothing more. My cup was running over.

After a week in the hospital with all the tests run and the reports in, it was evident that Pete's time was very short. Family members came to say their good-byes. One afternoon Ray Watts came with his barbershop quartet to sing a farewell to one who loved music so much and years earlier had his own award-winning group in Albuquerque. They stood around the foot of his bed and sang the old favorites. Although Pete had not spoken for several days, in his basso profundo he sang right along with them while the rest of us in the room stood there crying our eyes out. There was so much joy and pain all mixed up together.

On August 27, 2003, all life support was removed, and after three hours he took one last breath, and with a mighty shout he was gone. I couldn't even think of how I was to go on without this precious man, and I didn't try. He was at peace; there was no more pain and frustration, and I could only imagine his joy at meeting his Saviour face-to-face. It was so quiet. The absence of sound surprised me. I sat beside him holding his hand, that nice, big, capable hand, and I noticed that his fingernails were turning blue. How quickly everything changed!

There is so much to do when your beloved dies. I went onto automatic pilot, and the Schneiders were right beside me. They fed me, answered the telephone, and stayed for two days and nights. Bless them.

They went with me to the mortuary to identify Pete's body and sign papers. It wasn't until I saw him there that I really accepted his death. He was so white and so cold. Yes, he was gone from me forever. I was undone.

The memorial service was all I'd hoped for. There was comfort, compassion, even humor, and assurance for all of us that we'll meet again.

Adjusting to life without Pete was hard enough, but faithful friends and family were praying for me and that gave me the strength to keep on keeping on.

One of my least favorite duties is managing money, and now it was my job again. I was aware that my income would be smaller, but it was a rude awakening to realize by how much.

Pete carried the Survivor's Benefit Program (SBP) which was to provide me 51 percent of his base pay plus all of his his Social Security. When I went to Patrick

Air Force Base to learn of my benefits and responsibilities, I was rocked back on my heels to be told that the Congress, in their great wisdom, had cut back the benefits to widows and orphans to 32 percent of base pay and offset the SS to make the total income 51 percent. The effect was to reduce my household income by two-thirds.

I had some pretty uncharitable thoughts about the people who did that, and wondered how many of them ever read the Bible, particularly the Old Testament. Try Exodus 22:22-24. "You shall not take advantage of orphans and widows," it says then gives a long list of bad things that will happen if you do, ending with, "and your wives will be widows and your children orphans." Well, they do such things because they can, but there has been enough outrage that gradually they are restoring the benefits to the original commitment. After all, Pete never got a reduction in his premiums. Oh well, what to do?

Life settled down, and I was beginning to be comfortable with it. I didn't like it too much, but Lord, you blessed me with peace. I had a good routine of exercise, writing, and activities at Trinity. I was also beginning to enjoy solitude. I had never been comfortable with it before, but now I found it to be a real friend. In my contemplation I could give thanks for everything, even the pain. I had a delightful month-long trip to New Zealand —thank heaven for frequent flyer miles. Home once more I had settled down to working on the book about my life with Pete, when Hurricane Frances paid us a visit.

Lord, what are you thinkin'? Haven't I had enough? You took Pete away, reduced my income, then just when I'm getting it together again, my condo is destroyed. You could have kept away the twister that tore off my roof, but you allowed it. Water poured in, ceilings fell, and the mold began to grow in big, black blotches! The place was uninhabitable. Friends came from Trinity and packed up all that could be saved. Another member sent his truck for my household goods and gave me free storage for as long as necessary. How wonderful that was. I could hardly grasp it. I was surrounded with generosity and kindness. Anne came to give me moral and physical support, and Pete's daughter, Bonnie, came to help too.

The Daleys insisted on having me stay with them as long as necessary and made me feel completely at home, giving me shelter and love.

So, Lord, tell me what are you thinkin'? One by one you've peeled away all my layers of protection— my husband, a big portion of my income, my solitude, and my home. I feel like you've yanked me out of my secure little nest and dumped me on my head! It hurts, Lord. It hurts a lot.

I'm told that when one door is closed another will open. You have been very patient, so now I'll wait to see what you have in store for me. Pete loved Jeremiah 29:11, "For I know the plans I have for you, says the Lord, plans for good and not of evil, to give you a future and a hope." And my favorite is Isaiah 26:3, "For I will keep him in perfect peace whose heart is stayed on me, for he trusteth in me."

After the Saturday wedding of grandson Clay Staley last October, all the guests shared breakfast in the hotel lobby on Sunday morning. Wayne Collier, a cousin, came up to me and pinned my arms firmly to my sides with both hands, looked intently into my eyes.

"Fran, listen to me," he said. "I perceive things. Be very careful in all you do. You have a wonderful life ahead of you, but *be careful.*" I look forward to my future with great expectation and hope.

Here I am with a condo to refurbish after the association finally got the roof back on, but redoing the interior will take a lot more money than I have, even with a Small Business Administration (SBA) loan. So once again I'm helpless, Lord, but you are not. "The cattle on a thousand hills" belong to you, so if all that gets done, you'll have to do it. What an exciting prospect!

Before the hurricane a begonia started growing right by my front door. I don't know how it got there;

perhaps a bird dropped a seed, and it took root. At first there were just leaves, but now it's flowering for the second time. Today I counted twelve shoots, the tallest about eighteen inches high and topped with a cluster of delicate pink blossoms. In the midst of destruction it goes bravely on, blooming its little head off and giving me courage every time I look at it. Thank you, Lord, for such a gift, a foretelling of new life for me rising out of the ashes.

The Eagle and the Egret

Fran L. Peterson